MUSLIM TRIBESMEN AND THE COLONIAL ENCOUNTER
IN FICTION AND ON FILM

# Muslim Tribesmen
# and the Colonial Encounter
# in Fiction and on Film

DAVID M. HART

§

Het Spinhuis
2001

```
809.9 H325m

Hart, David M.

Muslim tribesmen and the
 colonial encounter in
```

ISBN 90-5589-205-X

© 2001, Het Spinhuis Amsterdam

No part of this publication may be reproduced or transmitted in any form or by any means, electronic or mechanical, including photocopy, recording, or any information storage and retrieval system, without permission of the copyright owner.

Cover image (photograph):   David Hart
Cover design:               Ruparo Amsterdam
Lay-out:                    Hanneke Kossen

Het Spinhuis Publishers,
Oudezijds Achterburgwal 185, 1012 DK Amsterdam, The Netherlands

# Table of Contents

Foreword by Paolo De Mas

I     Introduction    1

II    Fiction: Pakistan and Afghanistan    5

III    Fiction: Iran, Azerbaijan, Turkey and Somalia    13

IV    Fiction: The Algerian Jurjura    21

V    Fiction: Precolonial and Colonial Morocco    47

VI    Colonial and Postcolonial Morocco    85

VII    Films    111

VIII    Conclusion    125

Bibliography    127

# David Montgomery Hart
## 1927-2001

Just before the publication of this book David Hart left us on May 23th. It gives this book a rather sad and nostalgic dimension, because it marks the end of an impressive series of publications on Morocco and the broader Islamic world over a period of nearly half a century.

David Hart has been a leading ethnographer and conducted research from 1953 until 1967 in Berber-speaking areas of Morocco. In particular among the Aith Waryaghar in the Rif mountains in the north and among the Ait'Atta of the Central Atlas range, the Saghru massif and the pre-Saharan oases in the centre and south of the country. In between subsequent research in the Middle and Far East, he spent periodic return visits to both areas since then. He played a prominent role in formulating the structural-functionalist analysis of tribal systems in North Africa and the wider Muslim world. In his later work he turned more frequently to social history than to social anthropology as a disciplinary medium of expression and followed a comparative approach, which enabled him to reach for the specificity of tribal areas and systems in different parts of the Muslim world.

I first met David personally at a conference in London in 1979, organised by the Maghreb Review, but his fame had preceded him. As a freshly graduated geographer I had from 1974 to 1977 been member of a joint Moroccan-Dutch research project into the impact of international migration on the Souss regio in South Morocco and on the Central Rif, especially the provinces of Al Hoceima and Nador in the North. In Al Hoceïma we were repeatedly told of an impressive, berber speaking American researcher who knew the region well and who had studied the region exhaustively in the fifties and sixties. I managed to get hold of Harts magum opus: *The Aith Waryaghar of the Moroccan, the Etnography and History* (1976) of the most important single tribal grouping in Northern Morocco. Together with his publication *Emilio Blanco Izaga: Colonel in the Rif* (1975) it gave me clear insight in the customary law and in the socio-political institutions among this largest and notoriously restless key tribe of the Central Rif. But is did more that: I became hooked on this specific part of Morocco and kept regular contact with David Hart over the years. Moreover, his work on the tribal 'grass-roots' level proved to be also useful and relevant in studying the Moroccan immigrant community of approximately 300.000 people in the Netherlands. Nearly three quarter of them come from Northern Morocco, and a substantial part from the heartland of the Central Rif, more precisely the Ait Waryaghar, more commonly known as the Bni Urriaghel, whom Hart had studied on the eve of their massive migration to Europe.

The idea of publishing this book came during a visit I paid him in June 2000 in Garrucha, Spain, where he lived after his retirement. I was accompanying a team of the Moroccan section of Dutch National Television, who wanted to make a lengthy interview on his life in general, and more particularly on his research in the Rif. He really enjoyed the interview and gave answers to all our questions in his characteristic witty and repartee way. We talked for hours. He was pleased to learn that the second generation Rifians in the Netherlands showed interest in the history of the regions of origin of their parents.

It was perhaps this contemporary interest that made him show at that occasion the manuscripts of four books which were , in his own words '*stuff that sat around for years*' and asked me to help him '*start this material moving*' by finding a publisher in the Netherlands. So we did, and we are glad to have complied with his request.

*Paolo De Mas*
June 2001

# Introduction

It is unfortunate, to say the least, that the bulk of the average Westerner's infinitesimal knowledge of Islam and of Middle Eastern Muslim societies is derived from the image, by and large a highly negative one, which not only the film and television industries but the daily and weekly press as well as much of the publishing industry project of them. Even more unfortunately, his knowledge of those Muslim societies which are tribally organized appears to be totally restricted to vague associations of North African Berbers or Pukhtuns from the Pakistan-Afghanistan frontier charging down hillsides at French or British military encampments while brandishing swords and yelling *Allahu akbar!* This image, which goes back almost a millennium, as it has its roots in the Crusades, the first serious conflict between Christendom and Islam, was still thriving well over half a century ago during the final years of colonialism (for the film industry has been with us at least that long). Today, however, it has been largely replaced by that of the Iranian, Palestinian or Libyan terrorist who is given to planting car-bombs in or near airports and supermarkets. The political message behind the image is clear: negative even in the beginning, it might once upon a time have been meant to be regarded as something of a joke, but this is no longer the case. The negative image persists, and the object of the joke has become the enemy – especially of Europeans and Americans, and of Christians and Jews, who are all, nonetheless if paradoxically, in today's context, given in Arabic the very special and highly approved Koranic label of *ahl al-kitab*, 'people of the book'. What was ridicule in the first instance, in the face of ragged tribal attempts to combat 'progress', i.e., colonialism and its superior weapons technology, has become fear in the second, when the now decolonized tribesman catches up to turn the ex-colonialists' weapons against them. And Hollywood and the film and television industries, as well as even much fiction and reportorial 'fact', are all very much to blame for the perpetuation of these highly negative stereotypes: for the alleged cruelty and deviousness of the Arab has remained a constant factor throughout. In the present writer's view all of this represents the grossest possible misrepresentation.

However, my thrust in this study is more positive than negative. I have singled out a small number of films and works of fiction, directed and written both by Westerners as well as by Muslim natives of the countries and societies concerned, which by and large tend to show tribesmen, at least, as one admittedly small but nonetheless striking segment of the overall Middle Eastern Muslim population, in a more favorable light – for it is beyond our scope to cover peasants and city-dwellers as well. These novels, short stories and films have not been selected on the basis of any particular cinematographic or literary merit, both of which are criteria which I consider to be outside my anthropological purview or competence (and this even though anthropology today has managed to subsume numerous features and attributes of literary criticism), but according to the dictates of the perhaps more demanding criteria of historical, ethnographic and situational accuracy. This means, more simply put, according to what extent they seem genuine and have the ring of truth, or to what extent they reflect Islamic history and ethnography, to paraphrase Von Ranke, *wie es eigentlich gewesen (sein)*: for those which in my view do not ring true I regard as unworthy of comment. This latter category is, unfortunately, that of the great majority, and in this monograph I discuss, therefore, only a very small and select minority of films and works of fiction on the subject, ones which I regard highly both in terms of faithful depiction of the subject matter and in terms of their satisfaction of perhaps the most essential criterion of all: that of narrative, and the ability to tell a good story, one which is effectively supported with the relevant and accurate ethnographic and/or historical detail.

I do this not only to keep the study within reasonable limits in terms of length but again because only such a minuscule percentage of the enormous overall output even merits mention. A further observation is that, conversely, I make no claims to exhaustiveness, and there are no doubt a good many worthwhile films and novels of which I am unaware. But I believe the selections to follow may be regarded as the best of what is representative in the domain in question. I would add here only the caveat that although most of the films to be discussed are probably quite well-known, most of the fiction, on the other hand, is hardly known at all except perhaps to specialists. Indeed, most of the now abundant literature on literary criticism is itself irrelevant, in my view, because it is based upon literary rather than upon ethnographic premises. Ethnography and ethnographic content will, indeed, here take the place of literary criticism.

I shall therefore discuss the fiction first, and the order of discussion and analysis of individual novels selected will be, as much as possible, both chronological and geographical. I should add, furthermore, that I try to provide here as complete resumes as possible of the novels under consideration because it is only in this way that the quality of the author's ethnography may be determined: for in anthropology, context is all-important. The final point to be made is that, almost exactly as the best tribal ethnography during the colonial period was done by the British on the Indian (now Pakistani) North-West Frontier and in Afghanistan and by the French in Morocco and Algeria, so equally the great majority of the better fiction (irrespective of whether written by colonialists or by natives of the countries concerned) and films also comes from these two general regions, the Far Mashriq and the Maghrib. Morocco in particular stands out in bold relief here, a fact which is not entirely intentional on my part but which nonetheless reflects my longstanding fieldwork orientations. Certain exceptions, from Turkey and Iran, will also be examined, but the above caveat may be regarded as a general rule of thumb.

Last but by no means least, the issue of whether or not ethnographic novels may be regarded as *passe* or even as unfashionably detrimental to the 'postcolonial image', as some would claim (for example, Khatibi 1968), is in my view totally irrelevant and beside the point, which is that ethnography done and documented properly in the past can easily become very acceptable social history in the present. Indeed, and furthermore, as a dyed-in-the-wool ethnographer with long field experience in rural Morocco, in particular, I believe that a solid and sustained critique of the current postmodernist and deconstructionist 'anti-ethnography school' in anthropology is long overdue, even though it too may by now be water over the dam, and will not be made in this study. 'Thick description' is the very stuff of ethnographic fieldwork, and it is also at the core of the best ethnographic novels.

# FICTION:
# PAKISTAN AND AFGHANISTAN

No discussion of the ethnographic or historical literature on the North-West Frontier, on the region that is today the Pakhtu-speaking borderland between Pakistan and Afghanistan, would be complete without some mention of Rudyard Kipling who, despite the widely known fact that be was a leading spokesman for British colonialism and the Raj in India, was the first to put the region on the literary map. As Ahmed has noted, the figure of Mahbub ᶜAli, the Afghan horse trader in Kipling's novel *Kim* (Kipling 1901, republished 1980), is still, after almost a century, the most famous Pukhtun in English fiction (Ahmed 1977: 4-5), as well as one of the most sympathetic, despite the fact that in his role as a minor cog in the wheels of the so-called 'Great Game' – i.e., the contest for power in Central Asia between Great Britain and Imperial Russia in the nineteenth and early twentieth centuries –, he could, as an agent of Col. Creighton and the Raj, and as self-appointed protector of the renegade little Irish orphan Kimball O'Hara, for whom the novel is named, also be labeled a 'tool of colonialism'. Nonetheless, Mahbub's resourcefulness, forthrightness and courage, mixed with his native cunning and avowed self-interest, as well as his unquestioning faith in Islam, all combine to make Kipling produce a portrait (one which was reinforced by Errol Flynn's rendition of him in the 1950 film of the same name) of a very likeable tribesman whose adherence to his own cultural values evokes our admiration. The portrait of Mahbub ᶜAli, for instance, is totally unlike the much later and far more negative one of Sulayman, the homosexual 'Red Shadow', which Paul Scott gives us as the 'Bazaar Pathan' orderly of Col. Ronald Merrick, the egregiously reprehensible British Indian police officer in *The Raj Quartet* novels, specifically in *The Division of the Spoils* (Scott 1979: 200 ff.).

These two figures are of course extremes, although the other Pukhtuns who emerge in two of Kipling's short stories, *Dray Wara Yow Dee* and *The Head of the District* (Kipling 1987: 62-69, 164-81) as well as in his poems such as 'Arithmetic on the Frontier' and 'The Ballad of East and West', the latter of which was inspired by the exploits of a Pukhtun bandit of the period named

Kamal (Kipling 1977: 13-14, 99-103), may be regarded as between the two, but closer to Mahbub ᶜAli than to Scott's 'Red Shadow': for it is quite obvious that although Kipling shared enthusiastically in the generalized British Indian 'messroom folklore' about tribal Pukhtuns, he liked them, or those of them he may have known, whereas Scott equally obviously did not. *Dray Wara Yow Dee* ('All Three are One') deals with an unnamed Afridi tribesman who redeems his honor by killing his adulterous wife, and his subsequent burning desire to come to grips with and kill his escaped enemy and her former lover Dawud Shah, an action he is still anticipating at the end of the tale. In *Head of the District* (1891), the British district commissioner of the Khusraw Khayl tribe, who was locally well liked, dies and is replaced by a Hindu and Bengali *babu*. The latter is viewed with derision and scorn by the tribesmen, who under the encouragement of their religious leader the Blind Mulla of Jagai begin to raid villages and livestock in the plains once again, but are beaten back to the hills, with losses, by British troops. The mulla is discredited and then killed by the secular tribal *malik* Khuda Dad Khan, who comes in to throw both the mulla's head and that of the Bengali babu's brother (mistaken for the babu himself, who fled at the first sign of trouble) at the feet of the new, and once again, British, district commissioner as a token both of acceptance and of resumption of the *status quo ante*.

Some of Kipling's successors knew much more about Pukhtuns than he himself did. Apart from the late John Masters (whose novel *The Lotus and the Wind*, 1956, was clearly inspired by *Kim*), one of the best of these was an anonymous British officer who under the pseudonym of 'Afghan' wrote a well-constructed novel called *Exploits of Asaf Khan* ('Afghan' 1922). It sets out, in more or less chronological order, twelve exploits, in the same number of chapters, of a kind of super-Afridi named Asaf Khan. Most of these take place either in Peshawar or in the Khaybar Afridi Tribal Agency of the North-West Frontier Province during the approximate period 1910-1919, which culminated in the Third Anglo-Afghan War of 1919, although some move as far west as Jalalabad in Afghanistan and others as far south as the Punjab. Almost all of them are quite believable, and their ethnographic interest is considerable. The tone is set in the very first exploit in which Asaf Khan, his brothers and his father Qadir Shah adjust outstanding accounts with the more numerous members of the Wazir ᶜAli lineage in their own home village by inviting them to dinner and killing them all by trickery in the middle of the main course. From here on Asaf Khan continues to match wits and strength not only against his fellow Afridi but against trans-border Pukhtuns as well, and the number of casualties who fall prey to his rifle and Khaybar dagger mounts up through the book to an impressive level. His amorous adventures are also described in roseate detail, as is the way he turns the tables on a Hindu *bannia* or merchant. He becomes indebted to the British Col. Markham (who is no doubt modeled on Kipling's Col. Creighton in *Kim*, just as Asaf Khan is himself partially modeled on the Ghilzai nomad Mahbub ʿAli), and during World War I he saves the life of Markham's son in the Royal Flying Corps. There is a wonderful scene in which Asaf Khan, who has heretofore looked on airplanes as *jinn*-s piloted by ʿ*afrit*-s, realizes at last that they are just made of metal, wood and glue, and piloted by men; and then he gets the fright of his life when young Markham makes him a forward seat passenger in flight! Asaf Khan's loyalty to the Raj is, at least implicitly, questionable if not nonexistent, but it is, more specifically, transformed into a personal loyalty to Col. Markham, as a result of mutual eating of salt and saving of lives. It is this, of course, which leads to Asaf Khan's demise in the final exploit, when he and five Sikh sepoys together save a British frontier fort from 'treacherous' Pukhtun levies and Afghan army irregulars in the 1919 war, and die in the attempt to do so. The ending is consistent with the ideology of the Raj but not with that of Asaf Khan, pitting him as it does against fellow tribesmen, fellow Pukhtuns and fellow Muslims. But the events which lead up to it are for the most part quite credible, even if described in overly Biblical, overly Victorian English, while the ethnographic background, if understated, is nonetheless solid and good (and for a general Afridi ethnography, cf. Hart 1985, and Hart 1990, for an ethnographic summary). Less good, in another sense, is the guiding paternal hand of British colonial imperialism in the period immediately after that of Lord Curzon and the 'High Noon of Empire'. But it is unquestionably present.

The Kipling style and ideology in fact transcended the crucial year of 1947, that of Indo-Pakistani independence and partition, and it may even be discerned in a collection of fictionalized court cases by a Pakistani judge, Mohammad ʿAli, ... *And then the Pathan Murders* (ʿAli 1966), a good many of which are well-documented case histories, even though most of them are derived from episodes which happened in the so-called Settled Districts rather than in any of the seven Tribal Agencies proper. However, quite a different novel on the period immediately following that of *Asaf Khan*, the Third Anglo-Afghan War and its far more serious aftermath in Waziristan, 1919-22, appeared nearly sixty years latter in Wallace Breem, *The Leopard and the Cliff* (1978). The title of this book is based on a proverb from the Mahsud Pukhtuns of the South Waziristan Agency: 'On one side a leopard, on the other, a cliff'. Written in retrospect, Breem's novel seems far less sure about the goals of colonialism and empire; and it is also an excellent and highly perceptive recreation of a series of episodes which may well have taken place in Waziristan during the extremely tense period in question. This particular conflict was itself a result of quite unpredicted repercussions from the short Third Anglo-Afghan War of 1919, repercussions which, as it happened, were far more serious than the conflict which gave rise to them.

The title of Breem's book, which is possibly one that John Masters may have wanted to write but never got around to doing, is indeed apt. In the face of a rapidly snowballing Afghan *lashkar* or guerrilla war party which is in the process of involving potentially inflammatory Pukhtun tribal allies, Mahsud and Wazir, from the British-Indian side of the border in a *jihad* or holy war, a retread British army major, Charles Sandeman, at the advance post of Khaysora, is concerned about the loyalty not of his six subordinate British officers but of his 23 Pukhtun officers and noncoms as well as of a 1500-man scout force from a number of different tribes. Sandeman seems quite sure of the loyalty of the Khattak, Orakzai and Yusufzai contingents, less so about that of the Afridi, and not at all so about that of the Wazir and the Mahsud, who between them number over half the force and who are literally on the brink of revolt. (For a fine account of the social structure of these last two tribes and their role in present-day Pakistan, cf. Ahmed 1991.) It should of course be understood that in this essentially colonialistic context, 'loyalty' should emphatically not be taken to mean any sort of dedication to the British crown or Raj, which among Tribal Agency Pukhtuns, in particular, was of course nonexistent; it is understood more in terms of personal loyalty to an officer who liked them and whom they respected, who had trusted them well and whose bread and salt they had eaten – again, as in the case of the Afridi Asaf Khan and Col. Markham.

We are gradually given profiles too of some of the Pukhtun officers, especially the Mahsud Alif Khan and the Wazir Nadir (wrongly rendered as 'Nada') Shah, representing two neighboring tribes whose mutual enmity goes back to their ultimate common ancestry; while Ya$^c$qub Gul the Yusufzai and Dar Jan the Afridi are secondary. But it is at this point, while there is desultory sniping by Mahsud and Wazir hostiles outside the fort, that a young Mahsud scout murders the Afridi officer Dar Jan within it. The guilty sepoy, who turns out to be none other than Alif Khan's own son Zafr Allah, climbs up into the armory of the Khaysora fort before the decision is made that his own father has to shoot him down in order to prevent a bloodfeud, for the Afridi *subadar* also had some of his own agnatic kinsmen (or fellow tribesmen) serving in the militia. And the sentence is carried out. (As it happens, this incident is indeed based on a true episode, recounted elsewhere, although names have been changed: cf. Trench 1986: 17-18.) But while open warfare does break out, and the commanding officer, Col. Chalmers, is killed, the upshot is that nearly half the Pukhtun force deserts by degrees. Alif Khan and Nadir Shah, enemies though they are, come to a secret agreement over sharing the artillery in the fort once it is in tribal hands, and Sandeman, the second in command, is forced to lead a desperate retreat of the remaining 840 men back into the North-West Frontier Province proper outside the South Waziristan tribal agency.

Sandeman is full of self-doubt and unsure of his abilities as a professional soldier, but he grows steadily in stature, even while thinking of his pregnant young wife in India, as he leads the force back on the long march through blazing heat across a merciless terrain. Meanwhile the desertions continue and the sniping by tribesmen does as well. One early deserter is the Wazir officer Nadir Shah, whose knife-wielding fellow tribesmen now ambush and kill one of the four remaining British officers, Lt. Wynter. Another, Capt. Trent, is then killed by a sniper, while the doctor, Capt. Howard, is stabbed by a Wazir sepoy.

But a measure of trust, even if cool and calculating, develops between Sandeman and the Mahsud officer Alif Khan, a man who in his younger days is now revealed to have killed any number of enemies in feuds, as well as irate and vengeful husbands. He tells Sandeman that the reason the Mahsud, his own people, have deserted the force in fewer numbers than the Wazir contingent is because of *sharm*, honor – and he is aware of Sandeman's young wife's pregnancy. He also shows no chagrin, but tacit approval, when Sandeman shoots a Mahsud *jemadar*, Khiyal al-Din, for desertion.

Now, however, a large *lashkar* under the Wazir deserter Nadir Shah engages the remainder of the force in a major rearguard action, after which Sandeman and Alif Khan meet up with him personally, although by accident, when they are all guests at the home of the *malik* or headman of Banur Toi village. Later the same day, however, Alif Khan and Nadir Shah, who has been wounded in the arm, meet outside the village limits, in a confrontation which is electric with mutual hatred. Alif Khan admits derisively that of course he has tricked Nadir Shah and taken the spoils in weaponry from the fort himself, before disemboweling him with two swift and practiced strokes of his straight-bladed, bone-handled dagger.

At this point news arrives of a Mahsud *jirga* or council meeting at their tribal 'capital' of Kaniguram, which warns off the approaching Afghan *lashkar*, but which implies at the same time that if they take the Khaybar, Kurram or

Tochi passes, then the Mahsud will liberate South Waziristan without any outside assistance. But on 27 Ramadan, the Night of Power, which in Islam commemorates the sending down by God of the Holy Qur'an to the Prophet Muhammad, Sandeman's own Mahsud orderly Rafiq turns on him and stabs him in order to avenge the earlier killing (by Alif Khan) of his friend (and Alif Khan's son) Zafr Allah, for which he has blamed Sandeman all this time while pretending to be his friend. Sandeman is dying but shoots Rafiq dead on the spot – and he himself dies in Alif Khan's arms as they reach their final destination, a fort within the North-West Frontier provincial limits, where the colonel tells Alif Khan the news that young Mrs. Sandeman has borne her late husband a son to carry on his name. For both Sandeman and Alif Khan have, all along, been 'between the leopard and the cliff', in this evocative and powerful novel by an author who is thoroughly in control of his subject matter.

In our view, James Michener, in his novel *Caravans* (Michener 1963, 1968), misunderstood the nature of Afghan tribal tribalism and its relations with the central government (although the subsequent film, based upon it and shot in Southern Iran, with Anthony Quinn in the leading role of the *khan* of a nomad Ghilzai tribe who has made off with the American-born wife of an Afghan army officer, is not without its good moments). But both closer to the present day and to Afghan political realities is M.E. Hirsh, *Kabul* (Hirsh 1987), set in Afghanistan during the period 1973-79, from the quiet revolution and dissolution of the monarchy in that country in the first mentioned year, through the so-called 'Saur revolution' and on to the Soviet invasion at the end of the latter one. The story line centers around an upper-class, Dari-speaking Kabuli-American couple, ʿUmar Anwari, an Afghan diplomat, his Boston-born wife Catherine, their sons Mangal and Tor and their daughter Saira. It shows not only how they all respond differently to pressures but reveals the major tensions between the sophisticated foreign outlook they have acquired in schools abroad and their unavoidably deep involvement with Afghanistan and Islam. The end of the first section in 1973 sees Saira shamed and jilted by an American lover, while Mangal has turned revolutionary and is in good standing with the clique of the Prime Minister Muhammad Dawud that eases out King Zahir Shah in a bloodless coup while the latter is in Rome. Tor, meanwhile, has become a thwarted playboy, and by 1978, as a five-year student in Moscow, he hates the Soviets and has started to engage in black marketing and minor crimes, while Saira has become involved with a Soviet diplomat at the United Nations in New York.

But when the first Communist coup comes in April 1978 and Nur Muhammad Taraki takes over, has Dawud shot and proclaims the 'Saur Revolution', Mangal and his family are also executed, and his parents are placed under house arrest. When Tor hears about the Kerala massacre in mid-1979 from a fellow Afghan in Moscow, he comes straight home to join the *mujahidin*, the fighters for freedom and for Islam, finds that his father's old servant is a commander among them and that the top man in the unit, under the pseudonym 'Sher', is his own elder brother Mangal who was wounded but escaped after his wife and son were killed. He gets his family across the border in Pakistan, and then to New York, where they all discover to their horror that his sister Saira has unwittingly leaked information to her Soviet diplomat boyfriend. Tor returns at once to Pakistan in order to join the Afghan *mujahidin* ranks once again; and the book ends with his brother Mangal, or 'Sher', getting killed in action.

Hirsh's novel moves slowly at first but gathers momentum gradually and then goes like a bomb: one must just stay with it. The author has a fine nose for the niceties of Afghan politics, and one can hardly disagree with the unspoken verdict that if events in the country after 1973 had to be laid at the door of any one individual, that man was certainly President Muhammad Dawud. Nonetheless, for my own taste the book is too internationalized, with too many scenes set in Moscow and New York and not enough in Kabul or Peshawar. Although it is a good read and quite free from most of the usual Western value judgments (unlike Michener's *Caravans*), this same fact is precisely what stamp it as the work of an outsider. Some of the minor characters – such as Ghulam Nabi the Tajik family retainer turned *mujahidin* commander and Nur ʿAli the Ghilzai from Herat, the only real tribesman in the book – are well drawn; and Hirsh's strong suit is his high degree of political 'savvy' for the period in question.

Idries Shah, *Kara Kush* (Idries Shah 1986), is a many-stranded tale, by an Afghan-born author (although resident in England) who has heretofore written popular books on Sufism, which centers around the early years of Afghan resistance as led by the title figure, Kara Kush 'the Eagle', a onetime Kabul University lecturer named Adam Durrani (with a bow to the long-lived Afghan dynasty of the same name), from about 1981 to 1983. He and his girlfriend Nur Sharifi are joined by a number of other individuals, including foreigners of Afghan descent such as the Englishman Pendergood, in reality an Afridi tribesman named Pa'inda Gul, the Australian David Callil, in reality a Western Pukhtun named Dawud Khalil, and a Capt. Azambai, an Uzbek late of the Soviet Army. The novel's central theme is Afghanistan's struggle for survival, and woven into it is the denial by the *mujahidin* to the enemy of the 'golden hoard' of coinage looted by Ahmad Shah Durrani, the first sultan of the dynasty, from his invasions of India beginning in 1757. (I might add that the existence of bagfuls of Ahmad Shah's gold mohurs is almost certainly apocryphal, as I have never run in to any independent confirmation of it elsewhere. Equally spurious too, albeit still persistent and supported by the author, is the Victorian notion that the Pukhtuns are one of the famous 'ten lost tribes' of the Banu Isra'il.) Legend becomes so interwoven with history in this book that it is difficult to keep them apart – although of course it all makes for a good story, punctuated with scenes of combat against Soviet helicopter gunships from one end of Afghanistan to the other, as well as with frequent desertions of Afghan army units to the *mujahidin*. In sum, this is an entertaining if idealized account of the Afghan resistance by an author who is himself almost certainly a Pukhtun (one gem, on p. 132: 'An "Afghan salaam" is a stick of dynamite inserted into someone from the rear and then detonated...'). It also shows other minor tendencies, like taking a swipe at the Saudis ('the Kingdom of Narabia') in a way that only a fellow Muslim would dare to do. There is much in this book that is good and well told, but there is also almost as much that is trite and banal, which if the author had had any previous training in anthropology or history he might have avoided.

# FICTION:
# IRAN, AZERBAIJAN, TURKEY AND SOMALIA

In this chapter we move west to Iran, Azarbaijan, Anatolian Turkey, and much further southwest to Somalia. The first novel to be considered is Youel Mirza, *Stripling* (Mirza 1940). Although neither the author nor the protagonists of his book are identified in so many words, they are probably Kurds, and the book's location is unquestionably northwestern Iran. The story is about the social mobility of a refugee shepherd boy who rises to become *khan* of his adopted tribe. It opens with the escape of this boy, Jalal, from his own village (of the tribe of Hamza Beg) after having put a girl there in the family way. He heads for the mountains, befriending a dog which has also been ejected from a nomad camp for sheep-stealing, and together they then jump on an itinerant horseman and kill him. Jalal appropriates the man's horse and his excellent rifle, which indicates that he may have been an Iranian government official. Then he goes to a nomad camp where, although it is small and poor, he is taken in by its old chief Guzli Beg, who is unaware that his young and childless wife has become attracted to Jalal.

Jalal also befriends another old warrior named Hamza, and they go out together to steal sheep from a village in order to increase the camp's dwindling flock. On the way home Jalal kills another passing horseman with his throwing knife. He becomes popular with everyone in the camp save another client named Nadar Khan, who is jealous of his prowess – for his next exploit is that of capturing and trading some of his own sheep to the *kadkhoda* or headman of another village in exchange for two boxes of hashish for old Guzli Beg.

Jalal develops both courage and cunning in equal measure, as befits the sectional or camping unit leader he will eventually become; and there are further sheep round-ups, after which two surplus rams which refuse to fight each other are slaughtered for meat. He also has an amorous affair with Tamar, even while Sami, the daughter of Nadar Khan, of whom Tamar is extremely jealous, is attracted to him. His own tent is pitched right beside that of Guzli Beg, and as he enters the latter's tent to eat, people refrain from mentioning his name in connection with Tamar because they are all feeding on his sheep.

Then two sheep are missing or stolen, after which the nomads see what looks from a distance like a bear, and Nadar Khan shoots it. But it proves to be Tamar, in the moonlight, Jalal's great love who is far from her husband's tent; and she dies. Afterward the bones of the stolen sheep are found to have been eaten by wolves, two of which are then killed. Jalal consents to marry Sami although he will never forgive her father Nadar Khan for having shot Tamar. It is now that Guzli Beg dies after nominating Jalal Beg as his successor, and Jalal consents to take Sami to wife despite her father's misgivings. (In some respects this book is a novelistic precursor, in its knowledgeable comments about sheep and sheep transhumance, of Black-Michaud, *Sheep and Land* [1986].) Furthermore, as Jalal Beg acquires more sheep, he also starts to accumulate new members to his camping unit, through accretion.

At this point Nadar Khan is killed by a ram which has been purposely enraged by a shepherd whom Jalal befriended earlier and who hates Nadar. It was indeed Jalal Beg himself who passed this suggestion on to the shepherd in question; and thus we see him enlarging his own power base, indeed to the extent that the old warrior Hamza is able to secure for him the granddaughter of a neighboring chief, ʿAbdi Beg, as a second wife since Sami has not yet produced any children; and a heavy brideprice is paid for her in sheep. At this point the late Hajj Nadar Khan's wife, Sami's mother, produces a posthumous son.

Jalal, Hamza and the shepherd whom Jalal befriended earlier go out at night to steal wheat from villagers, but the latter open fire on them and they only get away with their bags half full. Then Jalal and his camp join forces with ʿAbdi Beg's camp, and he takes the latter's granddaughter Tallah to wife without any celebration. Jalal Beg soon assumes the *de facto* leadership of both groups, now amounting to some 200 men.

His next exploit is to take 25 armed men to rob a caravan in Azarbaijan. They lie in wait for several days and wisely pass up a 200-camel caravan with armed guards, preferring to attack one of only 50 camels, which comes by eventually, guarded by only eight men, who are all killed. Jalal captures the caravan and when they take the camels back to their camp to be unloaded, his men find sugar, wheat, rifles, pistols, sickles, copper trays, tea and tobacco. Jalal spends the first night with Sami and then they sacrifice two camels – and Sami learns that she is pregnant at last, only a month after Tallah, Jalal's second wife, has also learned the same about herself. Jalal still dreams of Tamar, but loves both his wives. Then comes the autumn move down to the foothills. Tallah gives birth to a boy and Sami to twins, a boy and a girl. And so it ends: Jalal Beg is honored by his people as a husband, a father and a fighter.

What is particularly good about *Stripling* is that it reverses a whole series of anthropological shibboleths about Middle Eastern tribalism: 1) a complete stranger and outsider comes in to take charge of a poor, small nomad encampment; 2) through repeated thefts of sheep from surrounding villages he enlarge's the camping unit's livestock base; 3) he becomes a favorite and protégé of the old *beg* and is nominated as the latter's successor on his death; 4) he builds up his power base through the usual Middle Eastern combination of boldness, opportunism, knowing one's opposition and looking out for one's own interests; and 5) his human allies, quite apart from the swelling of his flocks, are acquired through sacrifice, enforced obligations, debts., etc., in the course of which, it may be added, notions of classical segmentary lineage theory play no role whatsoever and are totally irrelevant.

We now move on to quite an amazing novel about Azerbaijan just before and during the immediate aftermath of the Russian Revolution (1917-21), by another individual writing under a pseudonym, and in German: Kurban Said, ʿ*Ali and Nino* (Kurban Said 1937, English translation 1971). This is the story of a young Azeri man and a young Georgian woman, both aristocrats, from Baku, who fall in love. But they are the products of two very different cultural and religious backgrounds: the Azeri youth ʿAli Khan Shirvanshir is a Shiʿi Muslim and the Georgian girl Nino Kipiani is a Greek Orthodox Christian. The author, who may himself have been an Azeri and a Shiʿi, describes the whole phenomenon of cultural conflict and clash in hundreds of different ways, and with consummate skill, with a keen eye for detail as well as a strong sense of humor. (The description of ballroom dancing as seen by a devout Muslim is not only amusing, but makes one see the matter from the viewer's standpoint, one of total shock and disgust!) ʿAli Khan's pride in his Shiʿi Muslim heritage and its links with Iran are especially well handled, and two points of climax occur in the book, first, when he gallops out on horseback after Nino, who has been abducted by an Armenian in a car, overtakes them and stabs her would-be seducer, and, secondly, after they are married, her shock when she recognizes ʿAli among the self-lacerating flagellants among the Shiʿa mourners for their martyr al-Husayn on 10 Muharram.

But their marriage survives even this. Nonetheless, it is doomed, as they themselves are, and after the Russian Revolution, when Nino has been packed off again to Tehran, ʿAli opposes the oncoming Communists in Baku, where he has sworn to die, with a single machine gun. He does indeed die – and it would be most interesting if this story were to skip another two generations and resume seventy years later in the persons of the grandchildren or great-grandchildren of the protagonists, in the wake of the Iranian Revolution, the collapse of Communism after 1990, and the resurrection of the ex-Soviet Central Asian Muslim autonomous republics. The work is in no sense tribally oriented, but its author's ethnic, cultural and religious pride alone make it worthy of inclusion and comment here.

The third novel to be considered in this section is Yashar Kemal's epic story of a Turkish bandit and his war against the injustices of local landlordism in the early 1920s, the early years of the Turkish republic, *Memed My Hawk* (Kemal 1961, 1981). The action takes place in the Chukurova (pronounced Tshukurova) Plain in the region of Adana in southeast-central Anatolia. ʿAbdi Agha is the cruel and grasping landlord (brilliantly played by Peter Ustinov in the 1978 film version of Kemal's book, which was unfortunately filmed on location in Yugoslavia rather than in Anatolia where it occurred) of five different villages, of which he lives in the biggest, Deyirmenoluk. Slim Memed (*Ince Memed*, the Turkish title of the book) and his mother Deuneh also live there, and like most of the other peasants, Memed has become ʿAbdi Agha's sharecropper. ʿAbdi Agha treats all the villagers uniformly badly, making them work long hours in the thistle fields, but Memed in particular is singled out for especially bad treatment and receives only one-fourth of the crop rather than the customary one-third. Memed is able to escape to another village where he learns that ʿAbdi Agha is detested by all and sundry, and that he and his wife were once stripped and robbed by a local bandit, Big Ahmet, who inspires both love and fear in his constituents and who, in line with Hobsbawm's famous model of the 'social bandit' (cf. Hobsbawm 1969, 1972; also Hart 1987, for a dissenting view), robbed from the rich to give to the poor. He learns this from Big Ahmet himself many years later, and he also learns that in the larger towns there is no single *agha* or headman, and that 'every man is his own *agha*.

In this way Memed realizes that ʿAbdi Agha is just one of many smalltime local oppressors; and it is at this point that Memed and the girl Hatshay declare their love for each other, despite opposition from both sides, as she is supposedly engaged to be married to ʿAbdi Agha's nephew. When Memed persists, ʿAbdi Agha throws him out while cursing and reviling him. Memed and Hatshay then elope. ʿAbdi Agha and his ugly nephew then beat up Memed's mother while an old villager tries to prevail on Lame ʿAli the tracker not to follow the lovers' trail; but he cannot help doing so once he is on it. The party catches up with both Memed and Hatshay in the forest, but Memed wounds both ʿAbdi Agha and his nephew with a revolver and escapes, hoping he has killed them. Hatshay is captured but Memed stumbles into the village of old

Suleyman, who then takes him up to the bandit Mad Durdu to put on his *tarbush* (which bandits even in republican times wore in the mountains, despite Atatürk's insistence on men wearing hats or billed caps) and join his band. They rob three foot travelers and five on horseback, of their horses, clothing and money. Memed shows that he can shoot but develops a strong antipathy to Durdu. News comes that ʿAbdi Agha's nephew Veli Agha has died of his wound, but that Memed only wounded his uncle in the shoulder; but as Hatshay is now a prisoner, she is charged with having killed the nephew.

Memed, now with Durdu's band, tries to make his chief realize that it is one thing to rob people but quite another to humiliate them publicly. They are caught in an ambush by Sgt. ʿAsim, but escape to take refuge with Yörük nomads, whom Durdu then proceeds to rob, especially his host Kerimoghlu. But when he tries to pull his trademark maneuver by stripping the latter of his drawers, Memed, Jabbar and Sgt. Rejep take Kerimoghlu's side but are unable to shoot Durdu, who escapes with the rest of his men. After a woman named Iraz tries to kill the murderer of her son (who is his own uncle, over an inheritance tangle), she is jailed with Hatshay and the two women become close friends. Hatshay's mother arrives with the news that Memed is the No. 2 man in Durdu's outlaw band, and the bravest of all of them. ʿAbdi Agha, frightened at this news, escapes to another village.

Two more men are then nearly robbed by Memed, but he gives them back their money and tells them to beware of Durdu. He returns to his village to hear of his mother's death, and now decides to go after ʿAbdi Agha and kill him. In so doing he enlists the assistance of Lame ʿAli the tracker whom ʿAbdi Agha had kicked out of the village earlier for failing to find Memed for him. Then Lame ʿAli finds ʿAbdi Agha in another village and pretends to be on his side. Thugs go to this village, where there is a long fusillade at the house in which ʿAbdi Agha is hiding; and they start to burn it. Sgt. Rejep dies of an earlier wound, but ʿAbdi Agha escapes again.

ʿAbdi Agha now goes secretly to see a certain ʿAli Safa Bey, who has become wealthy through playing villagers and brigands against each other. They strike a bargain: Vayvay village in return for ʿAli Safa Bey taking care of Memed. (There follows an interesting disquisition on the local social history of the Chukurova Valley: during the Ottoman period a number of Turkoman tribes were, over time, forcibly settled there, and with the defeat of the Ottomans in 1917-20 the region filled up with bandits and army deserters.) Memed, Jabbar and another man agree, with respect to the redistribution of land holdings, that the ideal for the region would be *mulk* or private property holdings for all, with no more landlordism, absentee or otherwise – while ʿAli

Safa Bey makes another deal with another bandit, Kalayji Osman, to liquidate both Memed and Jabbar.

An old man, Durmush ꜥAli, has the mistaken idea that ꜥAbdi Agha has died in a fire; so Memed wants to divide up all his property into *mulk* holdings and to burn the thistles, symbolically, as the end of serfdom-style tenancy and sharecropperism in the region. But then they learn the truth, that ꜥAbdi Agha escaped, and turn against Memed, who leaves with Jabbar. News is then brought by Horali, an ex-gardener (and now in secret a bandit out to get Memed) that Durdu has finally been killed by a crowd in a village where he was openly attempting to abduct women. Horali wants to lead Memed and Jabbar to see Kalayji, the bandit who is in ꜥAli Safa Bey's pay, and who is helping the latter to acquire more land. But Memed and Jabbar are aware of what is going on and in Kalayji's ambush Jabbar shoots Horali and Memed shoots Kalayji. It is now that Big Osman confers on Memed the sobriquet 'My Hawk' and brings him a large pouch full of money.

Memed is off again next day to the town to try to see Hatshay in jail. By pretending to be her brother, he succeeds in doing so. He throws his purse to her and to Iraz, after which they learn that the government is granting an amnesty to all prisoners. But Memed also learns from Lame ꜥAli that the women are to be moved to another prison, so he plans to capture Hatshay from the guards on the way. By this time Memed has already become a legendary figure, and he does not want Jabbar to come with him. It is only later that he learns, again from Lame ꜥAli, that no bandits who have ever come down to the plain from the mountains have managed to return home. Even so he ambushes and shoots the four guards who are leading the two women, and takes them up to the mountains on the horse that Lame ꜥAli has prepared for them.

Meanwhile ꜥAbdi Agha is very agitated, and petitions the local government to send in the army. ꜥAli Safa Bey tells him that an ex-bandit, Black Ibrahim, is now working with the police, who have instructed him to cut off Memed's head and put it on a pole in front of ꜥAbdi Agha's door, and to bring him in dead or alive. A police raid is then made on Deyirmenoluk, and another on Aktshadagh, but Memed keeps the forces of law and order at bay. A rumor now starts to circulate among the police that bullets cannot touch Slim Memed; and as a result ꜥAbdi Agha is in even greater fear for his life and wants to alert the central government in Ankara.

In the mountains during the winter Memed teaches Iraz to shoot but Hatshay will not learn. He comes back wounded after a shooting scrape with Black Ibrahim in which Jabbar draws the latter's fire so that Memed can get back to the cave where the women are hidden. The villagers now refuse to give ꜥAbdi Agha his dues as *agha*, though some still pretend to kowtow to him. Lame ꜥAli is then forced to follow Memed's trail in the snow, as he cannot resist tracking once he is given a trail to follow. In the cave Hatshay gives birth to a baby boy by Memed, and they then run out of ammunition. But Sgt. ꜥAsim refuses to accept Memed's surrender when he knows that Memed is doing it only to save his wife and son. At this point a blizzard wraps ꜥAlidagh Peak in snow, and news leaks out that Memed has perished in the drift. ꜥAbdi Agha and ꜥAli Safa Bey are overjoyed, especially as the latter has not yet sent off the former's telegram to Ankara. Memed is in fact still alive, but then a Capt. Faruq kills Hatshay in a police ambush. But Iraz takes the baby as a substitute for her dead husband and son further up into the mountains to be raised as a bandit.

The feast of Bayram and the governmental pardon finally come through, Jabbar goes down to surrender and Memed to shoot ꜥAbdi Agha. After he does so, he gets on his horse and is gone forever. But from then on the villagers hold a pre-autumnal plowing feast of thistle burning every year, and in the fire a ball of very bright light appears for three successive nights on ꜥAlidagh peak: it is the *baraka* of Memed 'My Hawk'!

We turn now to Somalia, for Gerald Hanley's novel *The Consul at Sunset* (1951) is obviously set in that country even though it is never once mentioned by name, and most probably in what was known in colonial times as Italian Somaliland. Somewhat reminiscent of Breem's *The Leopard and the Cliff*, although in my view not as good, its central characters are three British officers, Capts. Milton, Sole and Turnbull, who are posted to this desolate region after Italy's surrender before the end of World War II. They are as far from the European theater of war as they are from their homes and families, and each of them is conducting his own war with himself, so to speak, while all are trying to keep their charges, two tribal groups of camel pastoralists of obvious Somali antecedence which are given the names of ꜥUmar Bilash, the larger group, and Yunis Barra, the smaller one, from each others' throats. Only one of the officers at the outpost of El Ashang, Capt. Turnbull, seems convinced of the rightness of the British empire and of the worthiness of bearing the so-called 'white man's burden'. In Turnbull's case this is perhaps surprising, as he is the only one who has risen through the ranks and is an army officer pure and simple, while Milton and Sole are political officers and tribal administrators. Both of them, however, have clearly seen the writing on the colonial wall, to the effect that independence is just around the corner, while all three are affected, in different ways, by the desert landscape, its searing heat and its inhabitants who combine to expose their weaknesses. The story line is good and quite taut, but the ethnography, barring certain obvious points such as blood compensation being 100 camels for a murdered man and only 50 for a murdered woman, is weak. In addition, the Somali tribesmen who figure in the book are treated unidimensionally and without sympathy ('cruel, avaricious and vain, high-strung, cunning, quarrelsome, treacherous and fanatical'), both with respect to their primary concerns with their camels and with money, and with their detestation of both the former Italian and, even more, the new British colonial presence in the region; and they denigrate other, blacker Africans from further south as 'flatnoses'. Their elders had all served with Muhammad ʿAbdallah Hasan, the so-called 'Mad Mullah', in his long revolt of over two decades which ended only with his death in 1920; and their feelings have not changed.

However, Hanley's obvious dislike of Muslims in general becomes quite manifest through most of those Somalis in his novel to whom he assigns speaking roles, especially the whore Aurella (why, we might wonder, an Italian name?), a Yunis Barra woman who is Capt. Milton's bed partner but who nonetheless arranges his murder by a young fellow tribesman (a young man who had a local reputation because his father had killed two Italian officers) when Milton, driven by pressure, is about to turn a number of contested wells over to the ʿUmar Bilash, as well as the leading and elderly *shaykh* of the latter, Khalil Abukir. Milton, whose murder is blamed on the ʿUmar Bilash, is then replaced by Sole as political officer when Turnbull arrests and jails the ʿUmar Bilash chiefs so as to stave off their tribe's attack on the Yunis Barra. However, Sole is wounded and Turnbull's orderly Sgt.-Maj. ʿAbd al-Rahman is killed when an ʿUmar Bilash mob invades the El Ashang fort in order to liberate their leaders. While this is going on Turnbull torches their village, and only then discovers that Milton was murdered by the Yunis Barra. By now, however, the ʿUmar Bilash have attacked the Yunis Barra in a way which eerily prefigured the appalling later situation of civil war in Somalia (as of 1991), while the commanding officer of the region, Col. Casey, is like the consul at sunset in that although he would never admit that the sun might set on the flag of empire, he cannot help but seeing that by the end of World War II it has already started setting in the hearts of those who serve it.

# FICTION:
# THE ALGERIAN JURJURA

We now move much further west, to Algeria, and specifically, to its major Berber-speaking region, Kabylia and the Jurjura mountains. This region has produced two truly excellent novelists, both of whom wrote in French, both of whom had very sharp perceptions of the ethnography of their native land, and both of whom were inextricably caught up in the Algerian Revolution of 1954-62: Mouloud Feraoun (1913-1962) and Mouloud Mammeri (1917-1989). The former was murdered by the French OAS ultras just before the end of the Algerian war, and the latter, whose Berber sympathies made him a marked man on the part of the FLN after the 'Berber spring' of Tizi Uzzu (Tizi Ouzou) in 1980, met with an automobile accident which may well not have been entirely accidental. Both the two Moulouds, Feraoun and Mammeri, were novelists of exceptional stature by any standards. I have done my best here to provide synopses of their major works, beginning with Feraoun.

Feraoun's first novel, *Le Fils du Pauvre* ('The Poor Man's Son', Feraoun 1954) is obviously largely autobiographical, but at the same time faithfully ethnographic. Its first section, on 'The Family', is an excellent description of a Kabyle village named Tizi (meaning simply 'pass'), probably on the north slope of the Jurjura. It opens with a brawl that breaks out in the village square, where the *thajmaᶜth*, the village assembly, sits, after Bu Saᶜd n-ᶜAmr, with whom the 'author', a schoolteacher named Fouroulou Menrad (which is, of course, an anagram for Mouloud Feraoun) is on good personal terms even though they are in opposite *saff* alliance factions (into which every Kabyle village is divided), cuts Fouroulou on the forehead with a knife, quite accidentally, while in the process of making a donkey pannier. In the brawl, however, several people have received minor wounds when the village *amin* or headman manages to break up the fight, but Bu Saᶜd has been downed by the club of Menrad's uncle Lunis. Honor was saved, however, and the *dumman* or lineage representatives received a free meal from each *saff*. Menrad (or rather, Feraoun) leads us through the web of village kinship with a sure hand.

In the next section, 'The Eldest Son', Fouroulou, now eleven, has been an only son with three sisters, but then his mother gives birth to a second son, Dadar, and his father Ramdan, after getting sick, goes to France to work. Ramdan is the poor younger brother of Lunis who is ten years older. Shortly after Ramdan Menrad sends home his first paycheck, his son Fouroulou receives his school certificate at Ft. National (now l-Arba$^c$ n-Ath Irathen), 20 km. away from Tizi. Then Ramdan is nearly killed in a work accident in France, but is hospitalized, cured and comes home with indemnity payments from his foundry in Aubervilliers. But Ramdan wants to see Fouroulou drop his studies and go to work in the fields. However, Fouroulou is awarded a scholarship in order to get his *brevet*, after which he wants to enter secondary school to become a teacher (as Feraoun himself did in Tizi Hibel, where he grew up). But Ramdan does not have the money to pay for Fouroulou's board at the school dormitory in Tizi Uzzu, so Fouroulou and another boy are lodged with a Protestant missionary. And now the onetime goatherd rides to school in a car for the first time. Nonetheless, despite an excellent first year, his scholarship is, when he reaches age sixteen, not renewed for a second year. He has to come home as there is no more money. He is laughed at by his neighbors, but he persists and goes back to get his brevet. But should he fail his examinations for secondary school, he can then only go to work. He resolves secretly to do so in France if this is the case, for in Algeria he has only two alternatives: to become a teacher, which would mean economic ease for his whole family, or to become a goatherd again. His father counsels him not to be afraid, and on this note the book ends.

Feraoun's second novel was *La Terre et le Sang* ('The Land and the Blood', Feraoun 1953), in which the action takes place in another fictitious Kabyle village, Ighil n-Zman, in the mid-1920s. It is, Feraoun tells us, just like any other densely packed Kabyle village in the high Jurjura, with one difference: one of its inhabitants is a Frenchwoman from Paris who arrives in a chauffeur-driven car with her Kabyle husband $^c$Amr u-Qasi, who left the village fifteen years earlier (ca. 1910) and is only now returning for the first time. The consternation of the villagers at this sight is very well displayed, as $^c$Amr u-Qasi has not counted on the strength of local reaction to a *tharumith*, a Christian woman. His horrified and distressed mother Qamuma, in order to stand by her son, delivers the last word on the subject, as his father has been dead for a decade: 'Today we can receive absolutely anybody!' Despite their surface politeness all that the villagers want to know about $^c$Amr's long absence in France is how much money he has made – for labor migration to France has been a driving force in Kabyle life ever since the 1880s. His mother, too, has been reduced to penury and has not had anyone to look after her since the death of his father Qasi. However, she is seldom alone, as her house has become a meeting place for the women of the quarter, who keep her abreast of the local gossip and bring her food. At feasts, however, she tends to feel poor and left out, even though she has learned, as a poor person does, how to wait. Hence the arrival of her son ʿAmr is a good *maktub*, a good omen. Feraoun's handling of the relations between the new French 'Madame' (and Qamuma hopes that ʿAmr has not 'signed the paper', as she would still like to obtain a local wife for him), Qamuma and the other women is masterful, as is the advice that an older man gives ʿAmr about resuming his place in village life.

The women of the village are particularly fascinated by 'Madame's' yellow hair, but 'Madame' herself, however, and surprisingly, feels glad to have the change of locality and society even though as yet she knows not a word of *thaqbailith*, the local Berber dialect. She is, furthermore, obviously happier with Ighil n-Zman than her husband is after a fifteen-year absence, and sees it realistically as an adult rather than as her husband remembers it as child. When first in France he was under the tutelage of Rabah u-Hammush, his mother's patri-cousin and a member of the Ath Hammush, one of the two main lineages of the village, the other being the Ath l-ʿArbi. During ʿAmr's first year in France he was considered too young to work in the mines of the north, and he acted as cook for his group. But he soon found out that the Kabyles were the worst paid workers in the country, but that even so, instead of banding together, they brought their intra- and inter-village politics of *saff* rivalry to the workshop and were always fighting instead of sticking together. At this point, about 1914, his cousin Rabah has a work accident and is killed on one of the mine railroads, probably intentionally, by a Polish worker named André whose wife has become his mistress. The incident, however, is swallowed up by the beginning of World War 1, when ʿAmr is captured by the Germans and put into a forced labor camp. Released after the war, in 1922 he decides to go to Barbès where he meets his future wife, Marie, through the woman who runs the boarding house where he is staying.

Meanwhile, back at Ighil n-Zman, as it is believed that ʿAmr u-Qasi had a hand in the death of his uncle Rabah in France, he and his mother Qamuma are publicly renounced by the other members of the Ath Hammush lineage, the senior one in the village. ʿAmr's main enemy now is Sliman, Rabah's younger brother, especially because Marie or 'Madame' seems in fact to ne the illegitimate daughter of Yvonne, André's wife, by Rabah, her lover. (By this time André is presumed dead.) However, as of 1925, Marie can understand only the men at Ighil n-Zman because some of them speak French, whereas none of the women do, and she knows that she has to blend in with them. She wants seriously to learn the language, and some of the women begin to teach her; and gradually during the learning process she becomes used to her new life. There follows an excellent description (ibid.: 102-08) of the differences between Kabyle and French villages: in the former hardly anyone ever moves in or out, and everyone knows everything about everyone else, although appearances are always maintained insofar as possible, and although censoriousness exists, it is generally not voiced aloud. Specific examples follow.

One such is that ᶜAmr and his uncle Sliman suddenly meet in the street, both prepared (Sliman in particular) to hate each other, but instead they greet each other quite pleasantly and each then goes on his way. ᶜAmr's face in any case shows goodness and compassion. Ramdan, Sliman's father-in-law, who is not a kinsman but who took care of ᶜAmr once in France when he was drunk, talks to him privately in the cemetery, which he says is a faithful reflection, in the layout of its graves, of the position of the lineages in the village; and he also tells him that the old days when whole lineages exterminated each other in feud, or did so internally through vendetta, are now over, and that today there are policemen and prisons. He urges ᶜAmr to renew his relations with Sliman so as to nip in the bud any talk of vengeance, and to be on good terms with him, as nephew and uncle should be. ᶜAmr agrees to this, on condition that Ramdan make no attempt to make him appear a coward. (Sliman and Ramdan's daughter Shabha have been married for ten years, right after Sliman himself came back from France, but they have no children. Nonetheless, if the prediction of Si Mahfuz, the saint whom they recently visited, is correct, they will have one soon and have promised to sacrifice a sheep at his shrine.) ᶜAmr tells Ramdan to remind Sliman that he is the son of the latter's female cousin Qamuma and that he mourned Rabah's death more than anyone else.

Ramdan in turn says that he will keep the fact that Marie is the daughter of Yvonne by Rabah a secret at ᶜAmr's request, that land and blood (*la terre et le sang*) are two essential elements in anyone's destiny and that we are all insignificant in the hands of the Almighty. It would remain an open secret as Sliman might easily get it wrong by saying that his brother's murderer married his brother's daughter! But then Sliman and Shabha, with a fifteen-year age difference between them, start to become estranged from each other, especially as they have not yet had a child. (The case is related of Hmama, the wife of Hsayn u-l-ᶜArbi, who encourages her husband to take as his second wife his cousin Fatta, as they have not yet produced a child; and when he does so, she produces a child immediately and is then sent packing, dies two years later and the child grows up as Hmama's spoiled darling.) 'Madame', Marie, becomes very attached to Shabha, does not like Hmama, gets on fairly well with most of the other women and within a year is speaking fairly creditable *thaqbailith*. Meanwhile, Sliman, who is a real peasant farmer, plows the land at Tighzran which ᶜAmr has bought, as ᶜAmr himself can only look at it from a distance.

There follows an excellent description of the *thajmaᶜth* or village assembly meeting in the mosque on alternate Fridays, when nobody can agree on anything! ᶜAmr tells them, by contrast, how a French village meeting is conducted, suggesting that a roll call be held and that all rulings be recorded in a notebook. Even though this suggestion falls on deaf ears, it increases his prestige.

Shabha, Sliman's wife, and ᶜAmr look on each other almost as brother and sister, but over the course of time she thinks she may be falling in love with him. Then 'Madame', Marie, becomes pregnant. Sliman has to pay a visit to a *zawiya* leaving his wife Shabha alone, and Qamuma recommends that her son ᶜAmr sleep in their house as guardian. ᶜAmr and Shabha suddenly fall for each other, but ᶜAmr decides to take Shabha back to his own house, to sleep with his wife and his mother. In so doing he has a sudden vision of his late uncle Rabah u-Hammush.

Shabha suspects that Hsayn and Hmama know about the fact that she and ᶜAmr are on the verge of starting an affair. What they think others must be thinking about them is splendidly handled. Shabha and Hmama have an argument at the fountain in front of the other women, and Shabha calmly tells Hmama that yes, she has been surprised *in flagrante delictu* with ᶜAmr at least a hundred times, thus outfacing her. Hmama stalks off in a sulk. Sliman of course suspects what is going on but does not really know what to do. ᶜAmr's mother Qamuma thinks Hsayn and Hmama want to kill ᶜAmr and take over his property at Tighzran; and she tells Shabha that she should explain this to Sliman, with whom she does not get on, even though he is her cousin.

On market day a young and drunk member of the Ath Hammush tells Ramdan the father of Shabha that he has a she-dog for a daughter; and does he know what she is doing with ᶜAmr u-Qasi? Ramdan tries to beat the youth, but others grab his stick, so he rakes the young man's cheek with his fingernails before several of his own people remove the latter from the premises. The next day the Ath Hammush decide to ostracize Sliman, who has never been liked, but to do so in such a way that the rest of the village does not know about it, as well as to behave hypocritically with ᶜAmr u-Qasi. It then transpires that it was Hsayn u-l-ᶜArbi who incited the drunken youth.

Now ᶜAmr, Marie and Qamuma all start yelling at each other at home, the first two in French and the last in *thaqbailith*. ᶜAmr then faces Hsayn down at

Tighzran, and the latter runs back to the village. From now own his wife Hmama avoids Shabha and he avoids ᶜAmr. After this things calm down, while what ᶜAmr and Shabha thought might have been love turns out to have been merely affection.

Sliman then reaches a solution: to sell his property to ᶜAmr in a proper sale through a *qadi*, and ᶜAmr will then resell it all to Shabha, Sliman's wife, a month later. Thus all his Ath Hammush cousins will get done out of their share of the inheritance. But on the way home from seeing the *qadi* in town, Sliman realizes that Shabha may at last be pregnant – by ᶜAmr.

For the next land sale the *qadi* comes to Ighil n-Zman. Afterward Sliman sees Shabha and ᶜAmr talking together on an abandoned threshing floor below the house, and then he steals ᶜAmr's revolver from a large wooden *akufi* chest. He has a premonition about what will happen next day when they both go to the quarry. At the quarry itself there is a sudden explosion and a resulting landslide and ᶜAmr is very badly wounded, hit on the temple by falling stones. Sliman is also wounded, with a fractured skull as the result of the explosion. The possibility is strong that ᶜAmr and Sliman were fighting with each other when the disaster occurred, but this is not made explicit. In any event, ᶜAmr dies, and all the Ath l-ᶜArbi come to pay their respects to 'Madame', Marie, and Qamuma; and then, just as they do so, Sliman also dies. Shabha faints; and all is now in the hands of God: But 'Madame' Marie now knows that in her womb she has an heir. So on this rather contrived final note ends an otherwise first-class ethnographic novel, indeed, in my view, Feraoun's best one, even though I had the impression, even so, that the author, suddenly tired of two of his leading characters, wanted to kill them off quickly.

I will not discuss Feraoun's final novel, *Les Chemins Qui Montent* ('The Ascending Paths', Feraoun 1957) here other than to say that the love affair that he develops between ᶜAmr w-ᶜAmr – who is probably the son of ᶜAmr u-Qasi of *La Terre et le Sang* – and the Christian Kabyle girl Dahbiya (for there is a tiny minority of Christians in Kabylia, converted by the French White Fathers after 1900), though certainly interesting, as the book itself is, remains basically unresolved. But it is worth looking at Feraoun's *Journal* 1955-1962 (Feraoun 1962), which opens with a preface by Emmanuel Robles on its author's brutal murder, along with five companions, by an execution squad in Algiers on March 15, 1962, the day after its final entry. This work is certainly one of the best and most lucid statements on record of what it meant to be an Algerian Muslim in the final years of *Algérie Française*. After 132 years of being 'The Other', in the face of French ignorance, stupidity, lack of interest and assumed superiority, the Algerians had simply had enough. They were, for this excellent reason, determined to kick out their uninvited guests. However, Feraoun writes first and foremost as a Kabyle rather than as an Algerian, even though it is evident that he feels, and strongly, the existence of a national consciousness. The book is also an excellent running commentary, by a schoolteacher at Ft. National and a non-combatant, on the war as manifested in Kabylia, which was one of its heaviest theaters of action, one in which countless victims were slaughtered both by the French Army and by the ALN. But Feraoun makes it very clear that Kabyle sympathies, not least including his own, were almost 100 per cent behind the 'rebels' or *fallaga* (lit., 'bandits', as Feraoun himself often refers to them, using colonial discourse). It is also clear that he was not an active participant or combatant, as none of the ALN leaders of Wilaya III (Kabylia) is even mentioned. Hence I infer that he was not in contact with them. He had only sent his journal to Paris for publication the month before his death (his friend Robles having included the extra entries), but he was obviously gunned down by the OAS because of the clear and literate stance that he took against the injustices of French colonialism.

As Mouloud Mammeri (whose real name was l-Mulud n-Ath M<sup>c</sup>ammar) lived considerably longer than Mouloud Feraoun did, his literary output was correspondingly larger; but in terms both of subject matter and of quality they are readily comparable, although I would personally give Mammeri a slight edge over Feraoun. Mammeri's first novel was *La Colline Oubliée* ('The Forgotten Hill', Mammeri 1952), the action of which takes place in the Kabyle village of Tasga shortly before World War II. The major dramatis personae are the following: Muqqran u-Ramdan n-Ath Sha<sup>c</sup>lal is engaged to marry Tam<sup>c</sup>azzuzt n-Lathmas, locally known as 'Azi n-Ta<sup>c</sup>assast, the bride of the evening'. His cousin Mn<sup>c</sup>ash u-Vil<sup>c</sup>ayd (n-Ath Sha<sup>c</sup>lal) has a crush on Davda, the young wife of <sup>c</sup>Aqli, who has been to the engagement of another couple, Ibrahim and Sakura (known as 'Ku'), at which the former's family paid 10,000 francs and 6 sacks of wheat as brideprice, with the marriage to take place at the end of the autumn. Mn<sup>c</sup>ash regards <sup>c</sup>Aqli as a fool. The old village sorceress Naghnay thinks Mn<sup>c</sup>ash has drunk a potion and has become bewitched as a result, since his return from Fes in Morocco where he was supposedly studying.

There are two 'bands' of youths at Tasga: the Ath Ta<sup>c</sup>assast (Muqqran, Mn<sup>c</sup>ash, the Ath Sha<sup>c</sup>lal, etc.), all fairly well off, and the band of Wali, Ravah, Muh (who is Ramdan's goatherder), and several others, all poorer than the first lot, some of them miserably so, and all of them having left school early to go to work in France. Muh, the goatherd of Muqqran's father Ramdan, is an excellent musician on the flute and tambourine: his father has died and he sends money to his mother in another village, Bu Adda. Ravah who has worked in France calls the Ta'assast band 'the fascists'. Idir and Maddur, the brother of Sakura, make up the rest of the Ta'assast group.

Hard times have fallen on Tasga, however: there has been little rain and the springs have dried up, so most of the young men have gone to France to find work. There are many girls in the village, as the young men say that now just like *Irumiyen*, Christians, they have to find employment before they can get married. The people wonder if their saint Sidi Hand u-Malik has decided to withdraw his *baraka* from them and many younger ones even want to cut out the annual *timshrat*, the sacrifice of sheep or bulls at the 'Ayd s-Sghir feast following the month of Ramadan, or in spring.

The wedding of Ibrahim and Sakura is held just before the rest of the youths are called up for the army; and Idir returns home after having just missed getting into the Spanish Army, at the end of the Civil War, in 1939. Then come the nuptials of Muqqran and 'Azi, which breaks up the Ta'assast band, so Mn'ash joins Wali's band so as to become a part of the *sahja* choruses sung during evenings. At last they are all scheduled to join the 9th Algerian Tirailleurs at Milyana, going into the army as officer cadets for almost a year; and then they are sent home again when the Germans march into Paris in 1940. Muh the goatherd has also got married shortly before going into the army but he goes back to Tasga with the others rather than to his wife and mother at Bu Adda.

Muqqran's mother Milha and father Ramdan are worried that their son's wife has not yet produced a child, and the *shaykh* thinks that she and Davda, who is in the same position, should both go to visit the shrine of Sidi 'Abd ar-Rahman Bu Qubrin, a famous Kabyle saint, at Ath Sma'il so as to become pregnant. Tasga is once again full of its normal population, because the war and the German occupation of France have forced everyone to come back home. Unlike Davda and 'Azi, Sakura is producing children: two after two years of marriage, but her husband Ibrahim has to close his small business in western Algeria and come back to live on his earnings; and they become progressively poorer.

In a river crossing ceremony Mn'ash nearly drowns while trying to get Davda up onto the bank, and as a result he comes down with pneumonia; but he is strong and recovers. Then comes the excitement and dread, as well, of the pregnancy-promoting pilgrimage to the shrine of Sidi 'Abd ar-Rahman Bu Qubrin, with the *shaykh* and Naghnay accompanying Davda and 'Azi. Muqqran is so anxious for his wife 'Azi to become pregnant that he promises to sacrifice a bull to the saint at the shrine, a sacrifice that for him represents an enormous financial outlay, if Sidi Abd ar-Rahman can save her from barrenness, as she is still childless after three years. All of them then walk out backwards while facing the shrine, as they must always face it – save the *shaykh*, who forgets! Meanwhile, at Tasga, Sakura now has her third child, and goes to see ʿAzi, who gives her a pile of clothing when she hears how poor Sakura and Ibrahim are becoming: the clatter has now exhausted his meager capital, and has had to go to work on the road, under a foreman whose brother will lend him money only at exorbitant interest (prohibited in Islam), while Sakura becomes emaciated, sick and feverish. So further expenses must be paid, and the doctor, diagnosing typhoid, and hospitalizes Sakura for two weeks. Meanwhile ʿAzi awaits the *baraka* of Sidi ʿAbd ar-Rahman for several months and nothing happens. Ramdan starts to think his son Muqqran should divorce her. Naghnay now tells her there is only one recourse left to her: to attend the *hadra* or ritual dance of Sidi ʿAmmar, so ʿAqli and Muqqran both take Davda and ʿAzi there. There is dancing in front of the shrine both by groups of men and groups of women. The two wives enter the circle but make no requests.

Meanwhile the price of wheat goes up and then comes news of remobilization; and Wali, who has become a bandit in the maquis, returns there to resume his trade, a life that suits him well. A *timshrat* sacrifice is now held, and is led by the *shaykh*, with the meat of the slaughtered animal put up for auction. ʿAqli and Davda prepare to move to ʿAyn Bayda in eastern Algeria where he has bought a business. Sakura has by now had five children, and Ibrahim can barely feed them. She gives him money she has earned from carding wool. He asks his foreman for another loan, and to his fury the rascal has now put up the interest charge to 30 per cent, and he is desperate. So he talks to Ravah, who tells him how he can earn some money as a hired killer (this was common in precolonial and even in colonial Kabylia), by killing a man named u-l-Hajj (in Muh the ex-goatherd's tribe of Bu Adda) who has already killed his neighbor Umʿawsh, who had designs on the former's wife Kultuma. But Umʿawsh is reported as having died of snakebite and his brother Azwaw wants to take revenge on u-l-Hajj, through having him killed by a third party. Ravah tells Ibrahim that he could make good money by becoming this third party; but the idea infuriates him, and he refuses to do so outright. Then Ravah thinks that Wali would be the best man for the job. Wali is not happy with his wife Daʿdi, and in a contrived meeting with Kultuma (in which he and Ravah are disguised as *tulba'*, Qur'anic students), he is transfixed by her beauty. What happens to u-l-Hajj will be made clear presently.

## CHAPTER IV

Muh the ex-goatherd now develops typhus, and Muqqran has to go out in the pouring rain on his mule to get the doctor who lives 18 km. away at Ft. National. They arrive too late and Muh is dead. Muqqran is exhausted but he has to go another 40 km. to Bu Adda, soaking wet, to tell Muh's mother Tasaᶜdit the bad news. There he also meets Wali who under another name has come to kill u-l-Hajj. The rain has stopped but it is intensely cold and many paths are blocked by snow. Muqqran now returns to Tasga to help bury Muh and to find that his wife ᶜAzi has gone back to her mother, before he is recalled by the army.

Back in uniform, Muqqran is sent to Tunisia, where he fights bravely and survives a battle against Rommel's Afrika Korps; and at ᶜAyn Bayda he receives a letter from ᶜAzi who asks him to come back alive even if she is hardly his wife any longer. It is after this that he learns that ᶜAzi is finally pregnant – by someone else? And will she remarry? Here Muqqran's diary breaks off.

Muqqran, Mnᶜash and Maddur all set off for Tasga together with a driver, but the road is blocked by snow. Muqqran gets sick and delirious, and in his dreams he sees ᶜAzi, who keeps lamenting, 'I am your wife, why did you leave me?' At this point he keels over, wrapped in his burnous and crumples dead at the top of the pass. He is entirely alone at the time of his death and is completely covered over in snow when his cousin Mnᶜash, prodding carefully all along the trail, discovers his body three days later, and takes it to the Ath Shaᶜlal cemetery for burial.

After Muh's death his mother Tasaᶜdit has come to live at Tasga with Milha and Ramdan, Muqqran's parents; and nearly a month later ᶜAzi bears Muqqran's child, who is named for the father who died before his birth. Nonetheless, despite his name, he is called *Awlaᶜ*, Posthumous', by everybody; and Mnᶜash is especially hard hit by Muqqran's death. Maddur plans to remarry ᶜAzi in widow-inheritance fashion, but Ravah tells Mnᶜash that Wali will frighten Maddur out of fulfilling this proposal. He tells him the story of u-l-Hajj, whom Wali has gone to kill, on the road to Batna, as u-l-Hajj is now traveling as a hawker – and who therefore speaks Arabic as well as *thaqbailith*, which Wali does not. But in fact he does not kill him in his sleep as he had intended, and steals away. Mnᶜash on his return wants him to frighten Maddur, who he says has lost all Kabyle notions of honor.

Then ᶜAzi gets sick and, in Davda's presence, nearly dies. Maddur wants to look for another wife, as he wants to get married before his regiment is sent to Italy. Davda and Mnᶜash love each other, basically, but there is nothing they can do about it. Meanwhile Ibrahim has become desperately poor and decides to go to work in the Saharan coal mines, as ᶜAqli will not lend him money.

Sakura does not want him to leave, but he has no choice. So he goes off, and is joined by Mnʿash, on the way back to rejoining his regiment after a quick final meeting with Davda. Then Wali appears out of the blue, finds him, says he has seen him with Davda and could have shot them both. Sensing that this will be the last time, Mnʿash then bids farewell to his dead cousin Muqqran in the cemetery and goes off to war, never to return, so he says, to 'the forgotten hill' of Tasga.

Mammeri's second novel, *Le Sommeil du Juste* ('The Sleep of the Just', Mammeri 1955, English translation 1958), begins early in 1940. In an argument during a domino game at Ighzar village in Kabylia, Sliman as well as most of the rest of the participants and onlookers hope that the Germans will win World War II, but his elder brother Arizqi and cousin Tudart take the French side, as the French have built, schools, hospitals and other similar 'benefits' of colonialism in the region. Cousin Tudart in particular hopes so, as he is now wealthy and has more to lose. Sliman retorts by invoking the primary Kabyle virtue of honor, which he says means more than life or death, but Arizqi counters that honor is a joke; and when an elder, in the village square, tells him that Shitan, the Devil, is speaking through his mouth, he replies blasphemously that he does not give a damn either for the Devil or for God. The villagers are now up in arms against him and he only gets away through the intervention of Tudart. The same evening a delegation from the *thajmaʿth* comes to see his father to tell him to make sure that Arizqi commits no more blasphemy. The father finally finds his son in the courtyard of the mosque, and tells him to come home. He asks what happened, and Arizqi tells him quite frankly that he had said that God does not exist, for He can do nothing against logic. His father, he says, does not know what logic is, for his whole life is a denial of it, and adds that logic puts God in a dilemma so that He is caught like a mouse in a trap, a phrase he picked up from M. Destouche, the anarchist French schoolteacher at Tasga. He adds that the mere existence of evil discredits God. His father, of course, cannot understand or stand this incomprehensible behavior and goes to fetch his gun. He cannot believe that his son has read all this in books. He yells that he is accursed in his offspring, and Arizqi runs away from home when his father looses off a shot in his general direction. It transpires that while at school Arizqi wrote and translated letters sent to or home from France by workers there. He became 'everybody's Arizqi', *Arizqi-nnagh*, instead of merely Arizqi n-Ath w-Andlus. When the story opens he has just passed the entrance examination for the teachers' training college at Tizi Uzzu.

Arizqi's elder brother Muhand, who has worked in France under very poor conditions, has tuberculosis, and will probably die soon. Their father wants Arizqi to marry Muhand's widow-to-be Makyusa and take over their three children when he becomes a schoolteacher, while Sliman is to become a mason. The father goes to see the French administrator (*l-komisar*), who he finds speaks no Berber, only Arabic, and who wants to jail Sliman for having joined a 'terrorist' people's party, which was probably just a traditional village *saff* or factional alliance group. The administrator confiscates his ration card and then finds that he has not paid his taxes, and has mortgaged a field to Tudart, who has told the administrator all about him. He realizes on his way home that his world is falling in on him, and thinks that this is all due to an original curse which came about as the result of the Azwaw-Hand vendetta, Azwaw having been his own distant ancestor in the patriline and Hand having been Tudart's; and he dreams about the vendetta in question, the details of which I have recorded elsewhere (Hart 1994). He then forgives Sliman just before the latter goes off to Algiers, although Sliman wants to kill Cousin Tudart for having betrayed him.

In Algiers Sliman teams up with another Kabyle named Lunis, from whom he learns a little Arabic and French, and in whose company he obtains occasional jobs. On one of these they see the French foreman beating up an Arab shepherd boy because he has inadvertently let his sheep graze in the vineyard; so they rush in to beat up the foreman, Sliman probably for reasons of 'justice' and Lunis because he does not like 'the big bosses'. They now head toward Bwira (Bouira); and when Sliman asks Lunis about his tribal origins, the latter replies that he is an Algerian, and that Sliman will understand when he realizes that Rabah u-Himlat and the other members of the *saff* 'of the spines' are Algerians as well. He categorizes Arizqi, 'the almost *Arumi* or Christian', as a lost sheep.

At Bwira they find work on a farm, but the foreman is ᶜAqli, Cousin Tudart's son, who even though he does not recognize Sliman, hands him a letter which asks him to return home. Lunis says goodbye to him here, as with American troops about to land in Algiers he thinks things will change. So Sliman goes home to find that Arizqi has been drafted into the army and that his father has arranged for his marriage to Yaqut n-Tudart, the daughter of the head of the *saff* 'of spines', hostile 'for centuries' to the Ath w-Andlus. However, his sick elder brother Muhand says he will kill them both if Sliman marries Tudart's daughter, the daughter of the *amin* whom their father wants to kill, even though he knows that one must lick the hand that one cannot bite. There is a second Yaqut, however, the daughter of Rabah u-Himlat, far more attractive that Tudart's Yaqut, who is getting married to someone further away; and Tudart's son ᶜAqli is jealous because Rabah will not let him marry her. (It appears that Sliman would also have liked to marry her.)

It now transpires that the curse of the ancestors has continued to hold good: old Hand's grandson, also named Hand (for it is not only common but normal in most Berber-speaking societies to name boys for their paternal grandfathers), was an 'unbeliever' and a brawler like his grandfather, but was then killed in a *jihad* or holy war against the Christians (French) who attacked the Turks at Algiers, presumably in 1830. After the French invasion Tudart's grandfather was the only survivor, and he died a beggar. Tudart thus became involved in a fierce struggle for money, and hence through business dealings and currying favor with the administrator he obtained the concession to provision the whole district. He was hated by the Ath w-Andlus but knew that as they were poor, they would not have the courage to kill him. But he has to get rid of Rabah u-Himlat who stands for the old values and is in his way. The latter is made to wait for a good two hours when summoned to see the administrator, after Tudart reported that Rabah forced him to give provisions to a starving widow. Rabah resigns as village *amin* after a put-up petition from the Ighzar villagers asking that Tudart be appointed in his place.

Meanwhile Arizqi is called up at Bu Zariᶜa (Bouzarea). After the shot fired in his direction by his father, who considers him a heretic, he has not returned to Ighzar and has always gone instead to stay with an aunt at Tasga. Their old French tutor has left a letter for Arizqi and his friend Maddur. While still a cadet he is placed in the stockade for two weeks for merely trying to hold his rightful place in the dinner line against European cadets and for laughing in the wrong place at a radio program extolling France. Anti-Algerian discrimination in the French Army seems to be total, yet the incomprehension between Arizqi and his father's world also remains total. While drunk the night before the departure of the cadets for France at Mars al-Kabir, he flings around the bar-cum-whorehouse all the books he has been reading while in the stockade, and they are set alight, for the *iman* is not to be found within them. As the fire dies down he urinates on the flames.

Arizqi moves on to action with the 3rd Algerian infantry against the Germans at Cassino, and teams up with two Frenchmen in Alsace before they are both killed and he himself is wounded and hospitalized. Much of his experience is summarized in his letter-diary to his first teacher, M. Poire, and as a result of his war experiences he decides not to become a teacher himself. When the war is over in Europe neither Arizqi nor his batman Zarruq are anxious to return to Algeria as Zarruq's brother killed the foreman of his work gang, and then his father was killed by a stray bullet. Arizqi goes to Communist party meetings and has stupidly promised the party half a million francs. Now his brother Sliman wants to come to France, saying that it is up to Arizqi to marry Makyusa, for their father and their brother Muhand will do something very stupid if he does not come home soon to watch over them. Arizqi has no money and borrows some from Zarruq, who is now selling peanuts; he meets a casual French girlfriend before taking the train to Marseille; and then later, while wandering aimlessly around Algiers on arrival, and without money, he gets a bed for the night with a prostitute.

When Arizqi returns to Ighzar nobody wants to know where he has been. He is summoned at once to a family conclave, for his brother Muhand is dying and the *amrabit* or 'marabout' who is present has pronounced that Sliman is to marry his widow. Arizqi is relieved at this but sees that Sliman is stunned by the news; and he feels that life in Kabylia is nothing but a funeral, for everybody except Tudart. Yaqut n-Ath Himlat is there too, divorced by her husband after only a month. Tudart is holding a meeting next day and has taken over all the fields and property of Sliman's and Arizqi's father as payment for outstanding debts, including even their house, though he lets them continue to live in it: for Tudart sees everybody as either cunning, to be outwitted, or as simpletons, to be deluded. His son ʿAqli is about to marry the *qaʾid*'s daughter. At the feast that night all the members of the Communist party are arrested, as Tudart has betrayed them to the administration. As the feast is nearing its end, Tudart is shot in his courtyard, shortly after Sliman and the other party comrades are arrested and shortly before Muhand dies. Muhand said that Tudart had betrayed them all, so he shot him from his slit window, just before falling into a final coma.

Arizqi escapes, having had nothing to do with Tudart's death, but he is caught by French gendarmes with their Alsatian dogs. He sees himself, however, as the most responsible of all, because of his forged ration cards and the half million francs still owed the party from the women's Communist paper that he helped to set up while still in Paris. His father, delirious, finds Mecca in his own cell, while Arizqi himself is sentenced to twenty years in prison for a crime he did not commit, while the judge who has rendered the sentence prepares to sleep 'The Sleep of the Just', as the warden comes to take Arizqi away.

Mammeri's considerably longer third novel, *L'Opium et le Baton* ('The Opium and the Stick', Mammeri 1965) deals with Kabylia during the Algerian Revolution of 1954-62. In 1957, two Kabyles, Dr. Bashir l-Azraq and Ramdan, a teacher, are arguing about Algeria in the former's apartment overlooking the sea in l-Biyar, in suburban Algiers. The latter says that the French have even stolen the scenery away from the Algerians by putting all their boats in the sea, planes in the air and gendarmes in the forests, that the city is filled with blood, with torture by the police and the Arabs located in the ghettoes of the qasba. He is reading the colonialist newspaper *L'Echo d'Alger*, which Bashir never reads, and tells Bashir that he is closing his eyes and ears to everything going around him, especially as Gen. Massu has just taken charge of clean-up operations with the French paratroopers. Bashir counters by saying that throughout history the governing elite has always been small and the mass of the governed very large: the technique of the former has always been to use either lies or violence, opium or the stick.

Ramdan is working clandestinely for the FLN (Algerian National Liberation Front), while Bashir has a French girlfriend, Mlle. Claude Espitalier, whom he has just impregnated, and he feels he must urge her to get an abortion. He is a man of 1957 who does not accept the myths of his tribe (such as marrying within his clan), and he will not marry her because her illegitimate child will be spurned everywhere as a mixed blood and because he does not want to see another unfortunate brought into the world. He thinks about her, and it is as if she were entering the apartment, with her bourgeois and 'rose-bourbon' ideas and her world divided into the healthy and the sick and suffering. She has invited her aunt to come and stay with them, an aunt who lives in the country near Tours. Bashir hates the country, 'an invention of city people, with no flies, no dirt, no ophthalmia and no shit'. He is listening to French-slanted war news while waiting for Claude to return. A Kabyle boy recommended by Ramdan knocks on his door to ask him to come help his uncle who managed to shoot himself in the foot on a boar hunt; but it is late at night and he gives the boy the name of a colleague. The boy goes out, is arrested by French paratroopers, beaten and thrown into a jeep. Bashir phones Claude to tell her to come over, and then she and Ramdan arrive together. He tells her to send a telegram to her aunt saying that he has to go on a trip to his village, Tala Uzru ('Spring of the Rock'), and that they will write her when he returns. Ramdan hopes his tubercular lungs will let him live until independence. And while Ramdan and Claude are still asleep, Bashir leaves his apartment.

At Tala Uzru in the Jurjura, Muhand u-Sa<sup>c</sup>id has come to tell Smina that if she wants to see her youngest son <sup>c</sup>Ali, who went into the maquis two years earlier, she must go down to the Tizgi forest, as he will be passing through there next day; so she goes with her daughter Farruja, as <sup>c</sup>Ali is her favorite son, more than Bil<sup>c</sup>ayd or Bashir. She says that Bil<sup>c</sup>ayd denounces the *mujahidin* of the ALN (Algerian National Liberation Army) to the Christians, and that Bashir has become a doctor whose heart the same Christians have stolen. In view of this, what is she to do with the little money he sends her? In ten years he has not once been home. The men in the ALN file past, and ʿAli looks at his mother and sister but says nothing and is pushed into marching on. The women start to cry, and Muhand u-Saʿid tells them quietly to go home. Bashir hardly believed ʿAli when the latter told him he was going to join Wilaya IV above Blida and Shriʿa (Chrea). Lt. Hamid told ʿAli in the bush that if he wanted a decent gun he should go down to Blida and the Mitija to capture one, because shooting down a French helicopter always brought heavy bombardment in reprisal. So a week later ʿAli reappears with a new machine gun.

Bashir comes home to Tala Uzru, and is urged to play dumb when he meets Lt. Delecluze of the SAS. The latter tells him that in Algiers he was better able to pass around overlooked but that in Kabylia everyone lives in a glass house, on one side or the other, just as his brothers Bilʿayd and ʿAli are doing. And Delecluze gives Bashir a passcard. Then in the village square the latter meets his brother Bilʿayd, who tells him that after ten years in France he should not have come back to Kabylia. He says he can give Bashir ration coupons but counsels him to return to Algiers and not to play with fire. Bilʿayd only went to France himself for the first time at age 40 in 1946, by which time he was relatively well off, as he had worked hard and made his family do so as well. Farruja was married but her husband died in prison after an attempted coup and Bilʿayd virtually took over the care of the family before going to France when family fortunes began to dwindle. He sent money home but then began to drink, learning only later that his wife took their children and went back to live in her father's house. Then his own son saw him drunk on a bench in France, his son Wali who came to bring him home. There follows a big scene between them, the father who would rather live alone in France than be responsible for his family in Kabylia and the young son who gets angry at him, wants to take him home and finally does so. But Bilʿayd is soon tired of the Kabyles of his village and starts to frequent Delecluze and the SAS. He sends Wali back to the factory in Paris to work in his place. Ramdan, the son of Muhand u-Saʿid, tries to convert Bilʿayd to Marxism, but Bilʿayd talks only of Paris.

A meeting now comes up and Bashir soon hopes to meet, clandestinely, the FLN man who can take him to see Col. ʿAmirush, one of the leading ALN field commanders in Kabylia. The village *thajmaʿth* or assembly, however, now has a new feature: all the young men are facing the older ones, and people who in previous times would never have got up to speak are doing so now that Kabyle *nif* (lit., 'nose') or honor has become a thing of the past. The *thajmaʿth* of Tala Uzru has become a relay post for the orders of Delecluze as transmitted by a toady named ʿAmr. Guard towers and barbed wire are to be placed around the village while Tayyib, its most despised inhabitant and a notorious tattletale, becomes Delecluze's right-hand man. Bashir decides that he must be killed (although this in fact does not happen). Bilʿayd now tells Bashir that the family hero is ʿAli, that the young man who works in France to support the family is his son Wali, while their mother is fierce old tradition and Farruja is the widowed victim of destiny. He himself is the traitor, he says, and there is no place for Bashir, who should return to his patients in Algiers. But Bashir says he cannot do so now because of the police. He also says Muhand u-Saʿid asked him for news of his son Ramdan, and that he, Bashir, should go see him: to cure the ills of Tala Uzru a good diagnosis is needed as well as plenty of horse medicine. (Mammeri adds that at Tala Uzru there is neither a spring nor a rock, but this was the name of the original village toward the plain where the ancestors came from.)

Bashir sees Muhand u-Saʿid (who has a pass) after the curfew near the mosque, and Bilʿayd then comes to tell Muhand u-Saʿid that his son Ramdan has been arrested in Algiers. He tells his brother Bashir to leave the village through the south gate where he will find someone to lead him to Col. ʿAmirush. Bashir's ALN guide gives him a Lambretta machine gun after they get through the barbed wire. Five hours later the guide leaves Bashir with a forest ranger to whom he gives the password, 'Are there many boars here?' He is then given shelter. A group of *harki*-s in French pay come by but Bashir is safely hidden from them, and only the next night an old man arrives to give the same password and tells Bashir he has brought him a mule. The forest ranger had been thinking that Bashir was a French spy who had learned *thaqbailith* and wanted to kill him, but the old man said that Bashir is slated to organize the health service for the *wilaya*. Then they head for Ath w-Aʿban, where Col. ʿAmirush himself offers him coffee.

At Tala Uzru people complain during the day of being victimized by the ALN, but at night they are their brothers. Only a tiny minority are pro-French and they are hated far more than the French themselves. The war has emptied the village of its manpower, as those men who were working in France send money but do not come home. And Tayyib the turncoat reigns supreme, calling the people *sut Tala*, 'daughters of Tala', and hoping thereby to awaken their former arrogance enough to hit him, while Delecluze writes reports to his superiors saying that revolutionary wars must be fought with the same arms that the revolutionaries themselves are using. He thinks the

'Operation Jumelles' planned from Tizi Uzzu a terrible mistake. On its way up to Ath w-Aᶜban his column is ambushed, while Sgt. ᶜAli l-Azraq's group of *junud* or ALN soldiery, finding the mountains honeycombed with French troops, evaporates with the order to reappear at Ath w-Aᶜban in a week. But Ali's second-in-command ᶜAmr shoots some French soldiers from ambush, and ᶜAli's machine gun jams. He himself is then taken. ᶜAqli, the oldest man in the unit, cuts off his own left arm with a knife after it is broken by an enemy bullet, and is then taken to Dr. Bashir at Tigmunin. Here they are encircled by French soldiers and Bashir is wounded in the engagement. He is given a letter of safe conduct by ᶜAmirush to take him back to Algiers, as he needs a year to recover – so he leaves disguised as an egg-seller. And thus he returns to his girlfriend Claude in the apartment at l-Biyar. He spends a night there but just as he is about to depart for Kabylia again early in the morning he is arrested by a patrol of paratroopers, who on entering the apartment ask Claude if she is French. She replies, 'Yes, but *really* French', and the soldier retorts, 'Whore!'

Bashir is then taken to a paratrooper lieutenant who passes him on to civilian interrogators because he is so polite and learned and because he is wearing his best suit. The civilian police commissioner begins by reasoning with him: 'Operation Charm'. After the commissioner has departed, a Spanish policeman pushes Bashir back into his chair, and he cries out with pain, as his wound is not fully cured. What they really want to know, of course, is where he has been during the five months since he left his office practice in Algiers. The commissioner returns, still very polite but mixing in a number of leading questions. Then the 'heavies' come in and start to grill him, noting that shortly after he left for Kabylia Col. ᶜAmirush's health service became much better organized. Bashir then admits that he thinks his brother ᶜAli is in the maquis, after which the commissioner tells him that Ramdan has now talked, and that he himself must now do so or be confronted with Ramdan. He is left all night in he passageway with a number of others. The next day the commissioner tells him that Ramdan is sick in the infirmary and that everything he would have said is already in Bashir's dossier. Bashir says that if he is released he will then reopen his practice. The commissioner then tells him that it would be best if he left the country, when the Arab policeman who leads him out tells him quietly that his courageous friend Ramdan has not talked yet but that he is very sick.

After Sgt. ᶜAli's capture, he and ᶜAmr are taken blindfolded to a camp on the far side of Bwira, where Delecluze is waiting to get information from them on ᶜAmirush. ᶜAmr is badly beaten but does not talk. Then the soldiers all fall on him, and kick him around, finally loading him into a helicopter. He is taken up and dropped out, with no parachute, to his death. After this one of the paratroopers, Georges Chaudier, or 'Lynx-Eye', tells ʿAli to sneak out of the camp at night, that he himself will see to it that he has an opportunity to do so. ʿAli thinks he will be shot while attempting to escape, but the paratrooper genuinely lets him leave the camp unobserved. Then, thinking of all the trouble he himself will get into by letting him escape, he decides to escape with him. Later 'Lynx-Eye' tries to share his last can of corned beef with ʿAli but the latter refuses, saying it must be pork and therefore *haram*, forbidden. So Georges Lynx-Eye throws the can away. ʿAli then smiles and says the ALN camp is quite close by.

At an ALN training camp in l-ʿAra'ish (Larache) in Morocco, Bashir, through a Cmdt. Musa, meets Hubert, a French revolutionary who is disgusted with France and whom Bashir thinks would get on well with Ramdan. Then Bashir goes south to ʿAyn l-Luh in the Middle Atlas, where he rents a chalet, tells a girl who has just had an abortion not to drink any more, goes off in a car with another local Berber girl, Ittu, toward Khanifra, picks up a French hunter who rhapsodizes about the Middle Atlas, especially about mouflon hunting, who never stops talking, and whose wife calls him 'Tartarin de Ben Msik' after the Casablanca quarter where he lives (in fact a very poor bidonville quarter, which Mammeri may not have known, although he probably got the idea from an amusing joint Franco-Moroccan film, a updated remake of 'Tartarin de Tarascon', done in the early 1960s, about a quixotic French game hunter with a nineteenth-century mentality, who, totally out of touch with reality, is showed stalking lions in the downtown business district of Casablanca, while imagining that he is in a Kenya game park!).

Then they go to see Ittu's mother and her son Muha; although she herself is to be married in a month to a young man at the source of the Umm ar-Rbiʿ river, she wants to have a final fling with Bashir. After the feast that evening at her mother's place, Bashir plans to leave the next morning, but after he gets underway he finds that Ittu is curled up in the back of his car, determined to come with him. He says he will turn her over to the *qa'id* at Mrirt if she does not turn around and go home, but she stays with him, and in Meknes they buy things for her marriage. She insults a *talib* who is reading from a newspaper what she regards as lies about the 'neocolonialist' ʿAddi u-Bihi (the Berber ex-governor of Qsar s-Suq province who revolted against the authority of King Muhammad V in 1956-57, after Moroccan independence from France), whose trial is to start the next day; and she is insulted by the crowd in return. They go to Rabat when the trial begins, and then Bashir returns to his camp in l-ʿAra'ish. Cmdt. Musa tells him that there is a message for him from Col. ʿAmirush who wants him to come back to Algeria in two weeks. He returns to Rabat where the Berber girl Ittu is waiting for him. She tells him that ʿAddi u-Bihi has now been executed ('After the opium, the stick!') and that she must return home to her wedding feast. She is in tears, and hates Rabat and the city boys who try to pick her up. They go to Tangier and Tetuan and then head back to ʿAyn l-Luh, where she finds that her mother has covered for her during her absence by saying that she was with her elder brother on the other side of the forest.

Col. ʿAmirush has become a living legend, and even though at Tala Uzru Lt. Delecluze has been replaced by Capt. Marcillac, nothing has changed. Marcillac firmly believes that the ALN swims among the Algerians like a fish in the water, and he wants quick yes-or-no type action. The first thing he finds on arrival at his new post is a heat wave, then a forest fire (for the role of forest fires in the Algerian struggle against colonialism, cf. Prochaska 1986). They say that they cannot see the rebels in the fields because they are hidden by the olive trees, so Marcillac tells them to cut down the olive trees. So next day, pushed by the ex-beggar and now French toady Tayyib, who is reinforced by French troops and *harki*-s, the villagers reluctantly start to cut the trees down. They spin the job out to two weeks, and Tayyib laughs at them when they sit dumbly in the square with no more trees, no more bread and no more shame...

Meanwhile, Sgt. ʿAli l-Azraq and his ALN unit are marching toward the Akfadu forest. He and ʿAqli go to Tasaʿdit who is in charge of the hiding place in the village – and ʿAmr is her only son. From here they move on to Tala Uzru which ʿAli has not revisited for two years. Marcillac and Officer-Cadet Hamlet get their forces ready, while a large rebel forced led by ʿAmirush slips through their fingers at night. The characterizations of the French officers are excellent: Marcillac is the complete St. Cyr product who goes entirely by the book, while Hamlet is a Catholic choirboy who can only draw diagrams. Orders have come down from the colonel that if ʿAmirush has escaped it is because he has accomplices among the civilian population; and a list of thirty names is given to each officer with a suggested model of interrogation.

Bashir's most difficult task is crossing the Moroccan-Algerian frontier. He comes to a post south of Oujda from which a Moroccan flag is flying but which is in fact occupied by an ALN detachment. The French are aware of this and hence occasionally throw Algerian corpses back. Bashir is to cross with an ex-*harki* named 'Mosquito'. ʿAqli, the oldest man in Sgt. ʿAli's unit, can no longer remain on active service because of the loss of his arm, and hence is about to be sent to Tunisia on his final campaign.

In Tala Uzru, Tayyib and the *harki*-s herd the suspects down to the interrogation room. The men are interrogated first and the women hear their screams; and it is then the women's turn, with Tayyib and Capt. Marcillac doing the interrogation. Farruja has particular pressure applied to her, as she is ʿAli's sister as well as Bilʿayd's. After being heavily slapped around, she feels like telling them that yes, she takes messages, money and arms to the rebels, that there are five arms caches in Tala Uzru, one of them right behind the cupboard where she is standing. Tayyib cannot stand the hatred in the eyes of his cousin Muhand and starts to hit him. After five days the women are released, but Tasaʿdit, who has lost both her husband and her baby, taken from her by Tayyib, has now also lost her mind.

Bashir, disguised, gets a lift to Algiers in a vegetable truck and reaches his apartment to find a note from his girlfriend Claude saying that she cannot stand it any longer and has gone back to France, as well as another from Ramdan, saying he is still in hospital and will probably not live to see independence, so goodbye. A big demonstration of unveiled women with green and white flags is now coming up the street and French soldiers with machine guns are facing them. An announcement is made to the effect that they may demonstrate but not with seditious emblems like the FLN flag. This announcement is repeated several times, and Bashir nearly gets mixed up in the demonstration in which a number of people are killed. He takes refuge in the doorway of a house of an old Algerian woman.

Capt. Marcillac tells Tayyib to return the baby to its mother, but he says she has gone crazy. Tasaʿdit gives Tayyib her necklace in lieu of money which she does not have, as a *laissez-passer* for her and old Titi to go to Avizur. She is aghast when presented with Farruja's baby, not her own, but after playing with her, she finally gets her own baby back from Tayyib and runs off. She has also broken down and told Tayyib where the five arms caches are located in the village, as well as the fact that Bilʿayd is with the French by day and with the rebels by night. Word has come from the colonel that there will be an ALN meeting in the Akfadu forest which ʿAmirush is scheduled to attend, and the orders are to encircle it, with the help of a new company arriving next day.

Tala Uzru is now enveloped in silence after French soldiers come to clean out the arms deposits. Nobody appears, neither Tayyib nor the *amin*, and Bilʿayd wants to call a final meeting so that the whole village assumes responsibility for what has and what will happen. So they are called together from the minaret of the four-centuries-old mosque, and the *amin* leads off with a prayer just before the curfew starts. Then Tayyib appears and says mockingly that the captain believes they no longer have any reason for a meeting, while behind a wall women's voices are heard saying that one day the boys will become men and that the assembly will once more be one of men. Bilᶜayd proposes that a delegation of old men go to the captain to say that the village has separated itself from those in whose houses the arms caches were found – even saying that one of the guilty parties is his own sister. The *amin* raises the session by saying that the decision belongs to God and the Christians. Muhand u-Saᶜid then announces that he is leaving next day, and tells the young to take care of the village which has taken years to ripen, and some day they may speak of him to their children. Then he leaves – and no decision is taken.

That night, at the head of a convoy, Capt. Marcillac goes to head off the meeting of the *junud* in the forest. But the convoy is attacked by the ALN at dawn and is halted at noon by the heat in any case. Marcillac sends Hamlet out with some *harki*-s to dislodge a particularly hard knot of rebels. One-armed ᶜAqli is among the dislodged; and he surrenders, as does Sgt. ᶜAli, as they have run out of ammunition.

Ramdan, at Camp Bossuet, still has a raging fever, when the news comes through that ᶜAmirush has been killed. This news is then made official, with the Marseillaise sung over the radio (as of April 1959). Ramdan can hardly believe it but is sure that if ᶜAmirush is dead it is because he was betrayed. Nonetheless, he gulps and tells his companions that the revolution must go on.

Marcillac now wants everybody, including the pregnant women and those on their deathbeds, to assemble at the Du Tsilnin village square, where Tayyib tells them that they will all dance like beaten dogs. On arrival, Marcillac announces that as they have sheltered the enemy, they will all be considered and treated as enemies. But Tayyib renders much more hate into his translation of Marcillac's words. However, it seems that neither Bilᶜayd nor Muhand u-Saᶜid are present, though Tayyib brings out the two ALN prisoners, ᶜAqli and Sgt. ᶜAli, the leader of the group which attacked the French convoy the previous day, killing 71 men. He then throws a pack of cigarettes to ᶜAli, now about to die, in order to satisfy his last wish; and he tells him to pick them up. But ᶜAli replies that he does not smoke. Marcillac intervenes, however, saying that if ᶜAli does not pick up the cigarettes, he will fire into the crowd before shooting ᶜAli, while ᶜAqli tells ᶜAli that if he does pick up the cigarettes he will not die standing up. ᶜAli moves toward the cigarettes and is then shot down. Farruja sobs and Tasaᶜdit starts a demented ululation, which all the women in the village then take up. Marcillac feels as though their cries are deadly hailstones. He then has Tayyib tell them that ᶜAli's body will not be buried and will be given to the dogs. He gives them all one hour to evacuate Tala Uzru, which will then be destroyed by artillery fire, even Tayyib's house. The artillery fire begins in fact only three-quarters of an hour later; and then, while everyone stares terrified, the minaret of the mosque is blown up. Tayyib then thinks himself to be the last person in the village – but then he finds Muhand u-Sa$^c$id and implores his pardon, to which the latter laconically answers with Tayyib's favorite German expression, '*Raus!*' He then finds Tasa$^c$dit cradling $^c$Ali's body, which he wants to bury properly, now that he realizes how much scorn the French have for him. She places the body in the dust and Tayyib pushes her out by the Du Tsilnin gate. When Marcillac asks, Tayyib tells him that there is now indeed nobody left in the village.

In the final scene, Bashir writes both to Claude and to Ittu, telling the former to take his apartment, furniture and detective stories, but to leave the other books, and that she will be better off without him; and he tells the latter not to answer his letter but that she will know where to find him on the day of deliverance, as he wants her to come to him. And then, reconsidering, he tears up the letter when he realizes that the truth is not to be found either in opium or in the stick.

The final Algerian novel to be considered here is Rachid Mimouni, *L'Honneur de la Tribu* ('The Honor of the Tribe', Mimouni 1989), which opens with an old man talking into a tape-recorder and beginning the almost mythical story of his village Zituna, somewhere south and east of Algiers, and not far from Kabylia, by invoking the name of God the Highest, the Omniscient, the Creator of All Beings, the Orderer of All Events and the Master of All Destinies. Only a few of us, he says, still use our own language and soon nobody will know about the existence of the people of Zituna, now a century and a half old.

At this point Bin $^c$Ali the postman and 'Georgeaud' the café owner are introduced. The latter acquired his nickname by working in the foundry of Georgeaud et Cie. for twenty years, until after World War II. He says that what impressed him most about France was the fact that – unlike Algeria – there was water everywhere. However, the important event just occurring, as far as the local administration is concerned, is not the installation of a telephone system but rather that Zituna will become the seat of a prefecture, and will hence no longer be dependent on the larger nearby village of Sidi Bu Nmir. When this happens, Muhammad becomes the municipal councillor, and both Bin $^c$Ali and 'Georgeaud' now show themselves in favor of a new school, a lay one and not a Qur'anic one (which is particularly interesting and ironic in view of the fact that the Algerian version of Islamic fundamentalism first made itself known to the world at large in the same year that Mimouni's book was published). The new prefect is to be ʿOmar al-Mabruk whom everyone thought had died.

There is now a flashback to ʿOmar's grandfather Hasan al-Mabruk, a real troublemaker in his youth who ran off with the daughter of ʿAisa, but they settled down eventually, only to find that the Bni Hajar stole their cows, at which point he disappeared and may have joined the latter. His son Sliman, ʿOmar's father, grew up as an orphan in the house of ʿAisa's father and became a very hard worker. At this juncture a juggler and showman appeared, full of stories about his past exploits. He was always accompanied by his faithful bear (like an itinerant Turkish or even Russian juggler), which Sliman wrestled with every year. He won each bout until one year the bear beat him and he died the next day. His son ʿOmar saw his father defeated and the juggler prophesied that evil would now befall the village, given that nobody got up to help him.

So ʿOmar al-Mabruk returns after a long absence to insult the villagers and does not even inquire about his sister Wurida, who was furious at him for getting a job with a French Christian colon named Martial and seducing the latter's piggish daughter. But on ʿOmar's return he appoints Muhammad as mayor, and he is determined to change and modernize the face of the village, starting, for example, by allowing no more animals to roam the streets. The villagers are also accused of spreading leprosy and other diseases; and although they have done their best to avoid both the French colonizers and the FLN, they find that under the aegis of the latter they are even worse off than they were under the former. The situation is made worse when a large number of urban unemployed are foisted off upon them, for the villagers are convinced that all strangers, whether Algerian or French, bring evil in their wake.

After independence, which for the villagers is in no sense a panacea, their land is 'legally' attached to the state domain while their property deeds are declared illegible. They claim that their land has been spoliated simply because the tribe rose to resist the invader (and this is the first time the word 'tribe' is actually mentioned in Mimouni's text); but the judge of the prefecture declares that their request is juridically inadmissible, at which they agree that today's judges are as bad or worse than the colonial ones. They wait all day to try to see a lawyer in order to get some legal aid, only to find out that he has gone home.

ʿOmar al-Mabruk as prefect is harder on his fellow villagers than ever, and his has become the only authority in Zituna. The eucalyptus trees have been infected by the lepers in the region, and they and its numerous olive trees are all bulldozed down. Even though he was born in the village, ʿOmar brings nothing but disaster, even though he talks airily about building schools and hospital. 'Georgeaud' builds an enormous new house, however: he is doing well and wants to marry a twenty-year old virgin in spite of his advanced years. He does so and is then soon killed by the girl's lover when the latter catches them. ʿOmar al-Mabruk builds his own house in Zituna too, well protected by policemen and responsible FLN party members. Muhammad cannot now be reelected mayor, so ʿOmar puts his own man in office. He even decrees that the Ramadan fast be followed as indicated on the calendar and not as dictated by the new moon nor by the *ʿulama'* who have seen it. Indeed, many of the old men die off, including the *imam*. There follows a series of disasters, and finally the son of the local lawyer (who may in fact be Omar's own illegitimate son) accuses ʿOmar of all sorts of illegal actions. A scuffle follows, in which ʿOmar al-Mabruk is killed by the same flintlock or *bu shfar* that belonged to his grandfather. Mimouni has, in our view, misused the word 'tribe' when what he meant was obviously 'village'; but the irony behind the title, given the flagrant disregard for honor which is the novel's real *leitmotiv*, is apparent almost from the beginning. The so-called 'honor' of the village – or, indeed, even of the tribe – has been lost long since.

# Fiction:
# Precolonial and Colonial Morocco

Perhaps even more than in Algeria and in the Mashriq, some of the very best fiction having to do with Muslim tribesmen and the colonial encounter (because in the case of the Algerian Kabyles, their village affiliations were much stronger than their rather nebulous tribal ones, by 1954-1962), from the pens of Frenchmen, of at least one American, and of course and more recently, in the postcolonial era, from Moroccans themselves. This is not the place to discuss the colonial setting and scenario in Morocco nor even the notorious 'Berber Dahir' of 1930 that made the French preserve the customary law of Berber tribes in the Atlas Mountains in a deep freeze, away from 'contamination' by the Islamic Shari$^c$a law, until Independence in 1956, when it was promptly rescinded (for this and subsequent later developments, cf. Hart 1997[b]). Nonetheless, on the literary side, I am strongly tempted to agree with Abdeljlil Lahjomri, who suggests early on in an excellent study that the two French, and indeed European, opposing currents of hatred and enthusiasm for Islam have coexisted since the Crusades, with no room for indifference. Even more to the point, he adds that if there had been no Pierre Loti, there might not have been any Marshal Lyautey either, later on in the history of French penetration of the country (Lahjomri 1973: 12-13).

The work of Maurice Le Glay provides us with a good starting point for tribally oriented fiction in Morocco: full of colonialist paternalism and the myth of the 'Good Berber' vs. the 'Bad Arab', it is nonetheless also full of descriptive ethnography of a high order, unlike the later output, for example, of Marie Barrère-Affre (cf. Dugas 1985). We cite two examples, of which the first is *Récits Marocains de la Plaine et des Monts* (Le Glay 1922, 2nd Ed. 1948), a collection of short stories of which we will consider here, and fleetingly, only 'L'Amrar' ('The *Amghar*') (ibid.: 201-40) and 'Rabha, Fille de l'Amrar' ('Rabha the *Amghar*'s Daughter') (ibid.: 243-348). The first, which, divested of colonialist pretensions, is a very good story indeed, is the follow-up in detail of an episode in the early career in the famous precolonial leader of the Zayyan (or Iziyyan) tribe in the Middle Atlas, Muha u-Hammu Amhazun

Aziyyi (ca. 1855-1921), showing the beginnings of his development as a local strongman and the territorial increase of his own Ait Harkat section during his *qa'id*-ship owing to his alliance with the Sultan Mawlay al-Hasan I (1873-1894) as well as his fearful revenge taken on the Imrabten of Ulghas, under their saintly leader Sidi ᶜAli Amhawsh, because of their treachery. The wording of the story is such that one wonders if at least one of Le Glay's informants may not have been the same man from whom Dr. Louis Arnaud got much of his own material for his later and very lively chronicle on Morocco in the period of the *mhalla*-s, 1860-1912 (Arnaud 1952, and for a wider view of the same period, Burke 1976). The title of the second story refers to Rabha, the daughter of Muha u-Hammu who was married to a later sultan, Mawlay ᶜAbd al-Hafiz; but for at least the first half of it Muha u-Hammu is once again its principal figure and his relations both with the Sultan's guard and with the businessmen of Fez are splendidly described and certainly have the ring of truth. However, much of the plot of the story is unverifiable, though Muha u-Hammu's famous remark about *tulba'* or Qur'anic students being 'capons' is cited, and with gusto. The story takes Muha u-Hammu up to 1912 and the establishment of the French Protectorate over Morocco. Le Glay's second book here under consideration, *Les Sentiers de la Guerre et de l'Amour* ('The Paths of War and Love: A Moroccan Tale', Le Glay 1930), covers the resistance of Muha u-Hammu to the French, as well as his final years as 'the despot of the Zayyan confederation'. This work also contains an interesting portrait of a Zayyani, ᶜAmr u-Hsayn u-Bu Stta n-Ait Bajji, who wants to marry a girl who is also coveted by one of Muha u-Hammu's sons. The latter, naturally, and for economic reasons, wins her. In a rage, ᶜAmr u-Hsayn joins the French *mkhazniya* – even though his sister Duhu has married a Zaᶜiri and has remained loyal to Muha u-Hammu.

The next two novels to receive treatment here give me a real personal pleasure to report upon, as they were written by my old professor Carleton S. Coon, the first American anthropologist ever to have done fieldwork in Morocco. At the time (1926-28), right after the surrender of bin ᶜAbd al-Krim and the end of the Rifian War against Spain and France (1921-1926), Coon, then a graduate student at Harvard University, tried his utmost to cover both the physical and cultural anthropology of the Rif, and his pioneer thesis *Tribes of the Rif* (Coon 1931) still contains much of value and may still be read with profit. But the novels in question are *Flesh of the Wild Ox* (Coon 1932) and *The Riffian* (Coon 1933). I take as a ready-made and useful synopsis of the first half of the former book from another, much later work by Coon on the sociocultural anthropology of the Muslim Middle East as a whole (Coon 1951; 2nd Ed., 1962: 311-319, esp. 312-316).

In 1926 the *dshar* or local community of Iharrushen, in the Asht (Bni) ᶜAsim section of the Rifian tribe of the Igzinnayen (Ar. Gzinnaya) but close to where the latter borders those of both the Aith Waryaghar (Ar. Bni Waryaghal) and the Aith ᶜAmmarth (Ar. Bni ᶜAmmart), had only 13 houses (one of which was a mosque) scattered along both sides of the Saru Iharrushen stream just above where it joins the larger Aghzar n-Bayyu river – which itself, on entering Aith Waryaghar territory further north, undergoes a name change and becomes the Aghzar n-Nkur. Legend has it that the ancestor of the inhabitants of this community, one ᶜAbd r-Mumin (from whom they and the community derive their name, Asht ᶜAbd r-Mumin – or, as some have it, Imsaᶜuden) walked up the waters of the Iharrushen stream one afternoon just as the sun was setting, with his wife, cow and dog wading behind him. Silhouetted against the sunset he saw a mosque, newly built and empty, with its door open, standing before him. Faced with this miracle he removed his grass sandals and entered the holy place to pray. He and his sons hewed and walled terraces along the valley, felled some trees and planted others, and all lived peacefully until the valley was full, when men fell to quarreling over fruit trees, women and water. (In 1926, the population was 10 men, 13 wives, 19 sons and 15 daughters. Three men had two wives at once, as six out of nine of their fathers had been killed in a feud, and many of their brothers as well. Although the principal reason for widow inheritance, which is very common in the Rif, is to keep property in family hands, the death of husbands in feuds was formerly a contributing factor as well.) About 1890-1900 the Asht ᶜAbd r-Mumin were exiled from the valley, and I summarize here the events which led up to this.

It began on a winter night when ᶜAmar Aqshar ('the Scabhead') shot a neighbor by mistake. The Asht ᶜAbd r-Mumin had and still have neighbors, 26 families who call themselves Asht Tadmuth, after their ancestress who was one of old ᶜAbd r-Mumin's daughters – for ancestresses in the patriline are occasionally invoked to distinguish between half-brothers who had different mothers. It seems that the Asht ᶜAbd r-Mumin had contracted a marriage with another lineage group over the ridge in the next tribe, the great and powerful Aith Waryaghar (later to produce the world-famous bin ᶜAbd al-Krim). This Aith Waryaghar lineage, the Aith Haddu n-Mhand, located in the community of Tafsast in the Timarzga section, was in trouble. Sorely pressed, its members were besieged by a coalition of their neighbors and hence sent a messenger with a goat over the ridge. The messenger sacrificed the goat on the sill of the mosque so that its blood spattered on the door. This was a great ʿar or shame compulsion, which no honorable man could refuse. Hence both the Asht ʿAbd r-Mumin and the Asht Tadmuth, who shared the mosque, went to the rescue.

They lifted the siege but the enemy did not depart. One of the Asht Tadmuth, creeping out on a reconnaissance by dim moonlight, was spotted by the aforementioned ʿAmar Aqshar, who shot him dead. At this point an altercation arose. Shots were exchanged and with four parties involved it was hard to know who was shooting at whom. Si ʿAri, the venerable and highly respected community *fqih* or Qur'anic schoolmaster, who served both lineage groups as *imam*, was obviously the man to intervene and so he set forth from the huddled Asht ʿAbd r-Mumin in the direction of the Asht Tadmuth, only some twenty yards away. Unable to control their wrath, the Asht Tadmuth shot him. At this point a hush fell over the scene and by daybreak the two squads of kinsmen had gone home separately, carrying their dead. The Aith Waryaghar, over whom this trouble had arisen in the first place, and fearing to remain at home, went along with the Asht ʿAbd r-Mumin, who, outnumbered two to one, were glad of their company.

When the dead had been buried, the combatants found some fifty men gathered solemnly in council beneath their olive trees. These were the members of the *ashtarbiʿin*, the councillors from all the communities up and down the valley, who had heard of the trouble and had hastened to the spot to keep it from spreading (while enjoying in anticipation the meat of the fines which they hoped to collect). The moderator of the council was the Mᶜaddjim (Ar. *mʿallim*, 'master') Muhand, the wealthiest and most venerable of the Asht ʿAbd r-Mumin, whose position placed his newly made enemies at a disadvantage; and they lost no time in pointing out this fact.

It was clear that the Asht Tadmuth were the greater offenders. The council decided that both sides should pay bloodmoney to each other but that the sum paid by the Asht Tadmuth would be the greater. Both should also pay a fine to the council for having made it necessary to call them together. The Asht Tadmuth, however, demanded that the members of the Aith Waryaghar lineage should be forced to leave. The *amghar* or local notable and strongman of the next valley, that of Ikhuwanen, one Hajj Biqqish (later to become an unsuccessful rival of bin ʿAbd al-Krim in the war against Spain), agreed with the Asht Tadmuth and swung the council to this opinion. The Asht ʿAbd r.Mumin, however, refused, pointing out that their affines, whom they were protecting, had already had their houses burnt down and their trees felled, and might starve if they went home, if they were not shot first.

The meeting broke up without a decision and without the collection of a fine. However, Biqqish and the other leaders resolved to call together a greater meeting, a council of all five sections (in fact, all seven) of the tribal confederacy of the Igzinnayen, each consisting of several valleys; and thus three levels of deliberative bodies would be involved. The guests whom the Asht ʿAbd r-Mumin refused to eject were members of another larger and even more powerful tribe, as major intertribal trouble might easily ensue. Meanwhile, on the day before the Muslim feast of the ʿAyd al-Kabir (when, as Coon notes, everybody was bustling around as we do on the day before Christmas) the schoolmaster of the Asht Tadmuth appeared, with a goat and two other unarmed men. Approaching the Mʿaddjim Muhand's house, he declared that he had come to make a truce, and invited the Asht ʿAbd r-Mumin to come to the mosque and swear an oath.

After much deliberation and with some misgivings, the Mʿaddjim Muhand agreed, and set out with two of his sons. The Asht Tadmuth, as feared, had led them into an ambush. First the Asht Tadmuth killed ʿAmar Aqshar (the Scabhead), then the Mʿaddjim Muhand shot two of them and was shot in turn, through the head. One son, the Hajj Mhand, escaped, wounded in the foot. He crawled up on the mountain and his behind a rock. The next day, as the Asht Tadmuth left their houses all dressed in their new clothes, to go to the big mosque up the valley for prayer, he shot their schoolmaster and two others before his rifle jammed, which made him weep with rage.

Now the Asht Tadmuth laid a shame compulsion on Biqqish's men at the foot of the valley by slaughtering a bull on their mosque door, until finally the *imgharen*, the councillors, convened from hills and valleys, to sit like birds of prey at the scene of the slaughter. Many angry words were spoken before a decision was finally made. The Asht ʿAbd r-Mumin had committed sacrilege by killing men, however much they may have deserved to die, on the holy feast day which the Prophet Muhammad had designated as the end of the pilgrimage to Mecca. For sacrilege there could only be one punishment, exile. Leading a few thin cows the women of the Asht ʿAbd r-Mumin and the few men who remained climbed the path out of the valley, with the smoke of their burning houses rising behind them. One day they were to return, as we shall see shortly. In the meantime they lived in Lamta, a village outside Fes, with other exiled Rifians, caring for the olive trees of rich Arabs and dreaming of revenge. Not all returned, and their off-blond and light-eyed children and grandchildren may still be seen near the Bab l-Gisa gate in Fes.

## CHAPTER V

We come now to the second round, for the feud between the Asht ᶜAbd r-Mumin and the Asht Tadmuth was by no means over. In Fes, Hmid, the younger son of the Mᶜaddjim Muhand of the Asht ᶜAbd r-Mumin, persuaded a certain ᶜAbdssram of the Asht Tadmuth to kill his own kinsman Muhand Aqarqash ('the Freckled'), who had shot both his brother ᶜAmar Aqshar and his father the Mᶜaddjim Muhand, by promising to give him a girl from the Asht ᶜAbd r-Mumin in marriage and by selling him a rifle to do the job. So ᶜAbdssram went back home and shot Muhand Aqarqash as the latter was leaving the house of a peddlar with whose wife he had had an assignation; and he then sneaked back to Fes, while Muhand Aqarqash was found with his genitals stuffed into his mouth to show that he had been caught *in flagrante delicto*.

It was in their tenth year of exile at Lamta that the Asht ᶜAbd r-Mumin decided to return to the Rif, with rifles and ammunition. They arrived at Iharrushen early on a Thursday as the Asht Tadmuth were leaving their houses to go to the *suq*, the market, at Iqarruᶜan, and shot over twenty of them. In a return volley four were killed and the Hajj Mhand was wounded in the clavicle. In another battle in Ikhuwanen Biqqish's people at Thiddas in the Asht Tadmuth coalition lost twenty men and the Asht ᶜAbd r-Mumin only three, after which they decided to return to Fes. So far the Asht ᶜAbd r-Mumin had only lost 32 dead as compared to 68 among the Asht Tadmuth.

Years later the Hajj Mhand with his crippled son Muh Amzzyan and some others went back to Iharrushen to meet the old *fqih* Si ᶜAri and sacrifice a ram to Biqqish as ᶜar, after which they swore an oath in the mosque because now the *imgharen* appeared from all over the Igzinnayen forbidding them to return home. As a result of this oath, Muh Amzzyan stayed on in order to help rebuild their houses, and the Hajj Mhand went back to Lamta alone.

Muh Amzzyan's life was then saved by a certain Shaᶜib of Thiddas when he was attacked by a boar, and they both swore an ᶜahd covenant never to do each other harm. Then ᶜAri Aqarruᶜ ('the Big-Headed'), the brother of the late Muhand Aqarqash, threw a mad dog into the house of ᶜAbdssram who had killed his brother. ᶜAbdssram killed the dog but was bitten in the process and was shot in the Bni Krama country on his way back to Fes, after having turned completely rabid...

The Asht Tadmuth now attacked the Asht ᶜAbd r-Mumin on the roofs of their houses, with three of the former dead and three of the latter wounded, in a forty-day siege. In council, Biqqish brought up the desire of the Spanish to radiate out from their *presidios* in Melilla and al-Husayma Island, and Muh Amzzyan's friend Shaᶜib's bride-to-be was killed by a Spanish bomb dropped by a plane on the market. Shaᶜib vowed revenge and dropped hand grenades into the seats of three Spanish planes at Midar, before hiding in a cave. Here they got him, but not before he had managed to kill 43 of them. Biqqish now counseled all the Igzinnayen to patch up their differences and sent emissaries to the Aith Waryaghar, the Aith ᶜAmmarth and Muh Amzzyan to the little artisan tribe of Taghzuth to the west, in the Sinhaja Srir, where he shot a bandit named Yihya Azirmad ('Yihya the Left-Handed'), who had tried to rob him, along the way, and thereby gaining an extra rifle.

Coon now brings Si Muhammad bin Si Abd al-Krim into the story and makes a premature and, in my view, totally erroneous allusion to the latter's desire to set himself up as 'Sultan of the Rif' (Coon 1932: 234). Because there was already a legitimate sultan of Morocco, even though he was supported at the time by the French, my informants argued that bin 'Abd al-Krim wanted no such thing. Even though in early 1923 he established a *Dawla Jumhuriya Rifiya*, a Rifian Republican State, with himself as president, he saw it as a purely provisional and wartime measure (Hart 1976: 377; and for in-depth studies of the Aith Waryaghar and of bin ᶜAbd al-Krim and the two-fronted Rifian War of 1921-1926, cf. Hart 1976: 369-403 and 1997[a]: 23-76; and Pennell 1986, *passim*).

At any rate, Muh Amzzyan wanted the people of Taghzuth to go into bin ᶜAbd al-Krim's service as gunsmiths and leatherworkers. But now bin ᶜAbd al-Krim sent Biqqish a latter telling him to get his men to the eastern front to fight the Spanish, after the initial Rifian victories at Dahar Ubarran, Ighriben and Anwal in July 1921. Biqqish and bin ᶜAbd al-Krim then discussed matters in the presence of two *qa'id*-s or leaders of one hundred men from the Aith ᶜAmmarth. Biqqish said that bin ᶜAbd al-Krim should lead the Aith Waryaghar and that he would lead the Igzinnayen, and that after the war both of them should stand aside to let the councils decide what to do. Bin ᶜAbd al-Krim, however, said that first things must come first. He wanted to concentrate on winning the war and to follow up the Rifian winning streak in the east and invest Silwan, after burning the houses of the Aith Bu Ifrur (Bni Bu Ifrur) and the Aith Sidar (Bni Sidal) in the Iqarᶜayen (Qalᶜaya) confederacy for their loyalty to Spain. Nonetheless, in gratitude for having chased out a *harka* or war party under his Aith Waryaghar rival Tahar Nims ('the Ferret') out from his house under siege, an old Aqarᶜay man offered Muh Amzzyan, now himself on the eastern front as well, his daughter in marriage.

Relations between Biqqish and bin ᶜAbd al-Krim, never cordial, now became very strained, and one of the Aith ᶜAmmarth *qa'id*-s of 100 men now decided to throw in his lot totally with the latter. He suggested to Muh

Amzzyan that he do the same, as Biqqish was no friend of his. But Muh Amzzyan, more cautious, decided to adopt a wait-and-see attitude although the *qa'id* in question, ᶜAyyad, said he would kill him if he were to tell anyone about this.

The next episode occurs in about 1924, when some 25 Aith Waryaghar highlanders came into the Asht ᶜAru ᶜAisa section of the Igzinnayen to ask for Biqqish, as they knew that this section was against him. But they met up with a force of twice their size from Thiddas and Hibir, both in the Igzinnayen and both loyal to Biqqish. While they were in Hibir, the latter put potion in their food, removed their guns and set fire to the house they were in after having fallen asleep. Then the Igzinnayen went to Biqqish's house to report the matter to him only to find it under siege from the Iharrushen people and the Aith ᶜAmmarth. Four of Biqqish's men were killed, but Biqqish himself escaped to the mosque in Thiddas, where he stayed for three weeks while deciding whether to act or face destruction at the hands of bin ᶜAbd al-Krim. So he sacrificed a bull at the market at Iqarruᶜan and paid a fine of 3500 duros hasani, which the *imgharen* present distributed among their constituents, each man receiving a sum commensurate with his bravery in battle, while fifteen men received nothing.

Muh Amzzyan nj-Hajj Mhand was now summoned by bin ᶜAbd al-Krim to his capital at Ajdir in the Aith Waryaghar territory, overlooking the Bay of al-Husayma. The latter, 'no longer the schoolmaster', gave him a tongue lashing regarding the lies he had spread about him in Taghzuth (that he had once been a 'pimp of the Spaniards') but was pleased about the action he had taken against Biqqish. So Muh Amzzyan decided to join bin ᶜAbd al-Krim without reservation, particularly as the latter promised to make him a *qa'id* of 100 men if he rounded up all the Iharrushen men from Lamta to join his forces. He did exactly that, getting back to Ajdir via a lengthy detour in the eastern Rif. In the Ajdir quadrangle on his return he saw Biqqish sitting alone, while bin ᶜAbd al-Krim reminded him before conferring the *qa'id*-ship on him that he was now to be addressed as *Sidna*, 'Our Lord'. Then bin ᶜAbd al-Krim sent Muh Amzzyan back to Taghzuth to relieve the *qa'id* there so that the latter could go on to active duty on the Wad Wargha, the Wargha River, and the French front. Bin ᶜAbd al-Krim invaded the French zone in April 1925, one day before Muh Amzzyan arrived in Taghzuth. Muh Amzzyan, on arrival, was himself now instructed by telephone from Ajdir to proceed to the French front, while Biqqish was sent home to Ikhuwanen. Along the way, he conveniently died, through being given a glass of doctored mint tea, at Suq l-Arbaᶜ Tawrirt, the major market center of the Aith Waryaghar highlanders. In a battle with

French tanks along the Wad Wargha, after receiving word from Ajdir to withhold the attack on Fez, Muh Amzzyan was wounded in the leg after putting two tanks out of action with grenades, and the schoolmaster Si ᶜAri was killed. Muh Amzzyan now limped badly and was carried back to Iharrushen where his wife was in the throes of giving birth to a son.

Muh Amzzyan's leg was still no better in September of the same year when the Spanish landings took place at al-Husayma, forcing bin ᶜAbd al-Krim to move inland to Targist while the French moved north to occupy the northern Igzinnayen. A truce was effected at the Oujda conference (April-early May 1926) but nothing was gained from this except bin ᶜAbd al-Krim's decision to surrender to the French on the quiet at the end of May 1926. The Igzinnayen, furious at what they regarded as his treachery, joined the French and moved on to Targist themselves to capture him – while old Hajj Mhand died at Lamta.

Resistance was now over and both the Asht ᶜAbd r-Mumin and their erstwhile enemies the Asht Tadmuth were disarmed and their councils dissolved, while the French tortured or killed those still suspected of hiding arms. The Azru n-Tamza or Rock of the Ogress which overlooks Iharrushen was symbolically if not physically destroyed and Muh Amzzyan, beaten by an Arab jailer, was conscripted into breaking rocks after the blasting.

While *Flesh of the Wild Ox* is the 'internal' story of Muh Amzzyan nj-Hajj Mhand, Coon's second novel *The Riffian* (1933) is his 'external' story, under another name, ᶜAri Ushshan, ᶜAli the Jackal, his *alter ego*. Both names refer in fact refer to one and the same individual, Coon's old informant Muhammad r-Mnibhi from Iharrushen, and *The Riffian* chronicles his adventures outside the Rif. Both books begin with proverbs: *Flesh of the Wild Ox* with 'They that partake of the flesh of the wild ox grow in courage and he who eats of its brain becomes crafty', and *The Riffian* with 'Better a dog of the Ait ᶜAtta than Sultan under the French' (for studies on the Ait 'Atta of the Saghru massif, the Central Atlas and the pre-Saharan oases, cf. Hart 1981, 1984[a], 1997[a]: 77-149). When the latter book opens, the Asht ᶜAbd r-Mumin exiles from Iharrushen, led by the Hajj Mhand, were on their way south to Fes. The Hajj Mhand wanted to see if the *qadi* or judge who sentenced his brother ᶜAri Ashahbar, ᶜAli the Yellow-Haired, who had died in jail after stealing some of the sultan's rifles, could find work for them. Quite by chance he ran into ᶜAri's son, ᶜAri Ushshan the Jackal, aged four, blond like his late father whose name he had taken because the latter had died before his birth, and with a lady from the Middle Atlas as his unmarried mother. The Hajj Mhand took charge of him and took him to Lamta (which Coon confuses with al-Hajib, which is outside Meknes, toward the Middle Atlas, rather than Fes).

But in the decade or so preceding the establishment of the French protectorate, Morocco was in the throes of what was in effect a major civil war. The Shrarda tribe rose up against the sultan, Mawlay ʿAbd al-Hafiz (1908-1912), and took Fes (as Coon has it, which is inherently unlikely in view of the fact that the Shrarda were a *gish* tribe in government pay, one which furnished military contingents to him at all times), which was then, in 1912, retaken by the French Christians as the new 'protectors' of the country, with both Rifian and Imazighen Berber armies from the Middle Atlas converging on the city. But the French remained in control and in Lamta they broke young ʿAri's flintlock and shot his dog.

From early on it was the primary goal of ʿAri Ushshan to enlist in the French *Tirailleurs Marocains* in order to steal rifles so that the Asht ʿAbd r-Mumin could return to the Rif, which he had never seen; and he was adamant about it. So the Hajj Mhand finally agreed to let him go. He enlisted as an Arab, Muhammad bin Muhammad, from the Tsul, and his very first sight of Frenchmen filled him with loathing for Christians. But he was forced into a uniform (the year is now approximately 1916) and put on the train for Casablanca. He tried to jump off to retrieve a paper which flew out of his hand, but was held back by the other recruits. On the ship bound for France, he met another Rifian, ʿAllal n-Mumuh Azirmad ('the Left-Handed') of the Axt Tuzin tribe, who had also enlisted under the false name Muhammad bin Muhammad. He then stole a large pair of shoes from a sleeping black, as those he had been issued hurt his feet.

In Paris when the two Rifians asked for water or tea at a cafe, they were served beer, which tasted 'like the stale of mules'. Each of them went off with a whore whom he picked up in the cafe, and ʿAri Ushshan, after his own whore had fallen into a drunken slumber at home, emptied her handbag and took her money and her alarm clock, which went off and frightened him while he was on the street car going back to barracks. Back at camp he was instructed in the use and throwing of hand grenades, and immediately wanted to take some home for use on the Asht Tadmuth. He and his friend ʿAllal were now detailed to become sharpshooters. What in fact happened was that they shot seven French soldiers as well as the lieutenant who had ordered them to go into a special trench to shoot Germans, whom they did not really wish to harm as their sultan had made the *hajj* or pilgrimage to Mecca and was allied to the Turks. A shell burst, wounding them both and killing 12 Germans, whom they later claimed to have captured. For this exploit, entirely made up by them, they were both, on April 16, 1917, awarded the Croix de Guerre. At a party given by the French colonel for some American officers they sang in Arabic a song about 'Hajj Guillaume' (Kaiser Wilhelm II of Imperial Germany) who was about to castrate the French; but they were advised by an Arabic-speaking American officer to be careful where they sang it.

After the armistice they returned to Morocco but still had a year to serve. ʿAri Ushshan returned to Lamta, and when the Hajj Mhand asked him how many Germans he had killed, he replied, truthfully, 'None', and when next asked how many Frenchmen, he answered, 'I did not stop to count them but the gates of Paradise are not closed to me'. He arrived at Lamta just in time to find the Asht ʿAbd r-Mumin planning to return to Iharrushen. But the Hajj Mhand said that he himself could not return to live there because of his sacrilegious act of killing three Asht Tadmuth men on the day of the ʿAyd al-Kabir and that ʿAri Ushshan would do much better by serving out his final year in the army first. So the Hajj Mhand and the others returned to Iharrushen while Hmid and ʿAri Ushshan remained in Lamta. The latter went back to his army camp and spent the evening with a Berber girl from the Aith Ndhir, who agreed to marry him at the end of his service, once he destroyed her blue prostitute's ticket. He impersonated the captain whose orderly he had now become and won back his pay, lost at cards, in kind through taxing local *shaykh*-s. Then he went to see his girl l-Wazna, but found her with an Arab and partly black cavalry trooper, a guard of the *Qaʾid* l-Marnisi, whom he shot dead but not before he got a severe blow on the head from the latter's sabre. He needed trephination, which was performed by an army doctor without an anesthetic until Dr. Pagani came in to put him under ether.

For killing the Arab guardsman ʿAri Ushshan was sentenced in Meknes to seven years' penal servitude before finishing his term of enlistment, and was told by his defense attorney that if it had not been for him, he would probably have been guillotined. (It is not without interest to note that even in this very early work, Coon was deeply concerned about French treatment of Moroccans as inferiors, and his anti-colonialist sentiments come out strongly.) ʿAri was jailed and then put to work on the sandline, but eventually, as of the early 1920s, he effected an escape to the country of the Ait Mgild tribe in the Middle Atlas. The latter turned him into a schoolmaster, as according to his captor Muha u-Muha, he could not ride a horse. ʿAri Ushshan wanted to teach the Ait Mgild new ways of making war on the French, to snipe at them continually from shelters instead of leading wild cavalry charges against them. So combining the two techniques, they attacked a French post, killing all its legionnaire defenders, and capturing many rifles and a machine gun.

CHAPTER V

While ʿAri Ushshan became a *fqih* to the Ait Mgild, news filtered down that the Rifians, heretofore at war only with Spain, were now at war with France as well. He only heard how serious things had become from a French captain who had recently returned from the Rifian front. Most of the Igzinnayen had submitted except for a few valleys in the north. The captain realized that ʿAri Ushshan was both a Rifian and an escaped army convict when he discovered Dr. Pagani's trephination on his head; and he and his adjudant were about to take ʿAri away when Muha u-Muha shot them from hiding. But Muha u-Muha wanted ʿAri Ushshan to remain with the Ait Mgild as a schoolmaster and not to return to the Rif. So ʿAri put a knockout drop in Muha's tea so that he would sleep for at least three hours, and headed north on Muha's mare. At the gorge of Shikar he met an old man who told him that the region belonged to the 'Sultan of Pimps' (Mawlay Yusuf, 1912-1927, the grandfather of King Hasan II of Morocco) and to the French, and that the latter had offered to make him *shaykh*: '*Shaykh* of what? Of nothing! Better a dog of the Ait ʿAtta than Sultan under the French!' (Cf. Hart 1981, 1984, 1997[a]: 77-149.)

ʿAri Ushshan then went on to Taza, past Aknul and Bu Isli, where the mare he had stolen from Muha u-Muha fell off a precipice, so he had to shoot her. Then continuing north on foot, he went on to Iqarruʿan and up past the Thaʿrurth n-Tghujidh, the Noisy Mountain, and finally into Thiddas where a boy with a gun told him not to move any further until he could prove who he was. He did so and rejoiced when he finally saw his cousin (and *alter ego*) Muh Amzzyan again, now very lame as the result of having been wounded in the campaign along the Wad Wargha. He then went on to the French post at Buridh (Boured) leading his cow and pretending she was his only possession met some drunken German legionnaires there, milked the cow in a moronic fashion, and when the legionnaires went to sleep, he wrapped up five rifles in each of two jillabas and walked the cow back to Iharrushen carrying them. Here at home again, he planned to marry the 'third Fatima', for women now outnumbered men in the Rif, as so many of them had been killed in the war. To Muh Amzzyan he also confessed that he himself would like one of the ten rifles he brought back with its stock inlaid in a leaflike silver design.

It is not without interest, finally, to note what Coon himself said about these books nearly fifty years later, in 1980, the year before his death, in a letter to his granddaughter (Coon 1981: 89): 'I can only tell you how it felt to be writing about North Africa in the 1930s by telling you what happened. Muhammad r-Mnibhi went home (from Cambridge, Massachusetts, where he had spent a year with the Coons) to his death in 1929... In 1928-29 I had debriefed r-Mnibhi of all the information he could tell me, as well as what he had told me in Morocco and (having written my Ph.D. thesis in 1928) I rewrote it as *Tribes of the Rif* and I put the saga of the Asht ʿAbd r-Mumin (Ulad ʿAbd l-Mumin) into two books, both about r-Mnibhi. In *Flesh of the Wild Ox* he was Muh Amzzyan (Moh Umzien) ... I just wrote the book. It came out of my head and heart. I was like a medium. I never changed a word except when Mr. Morrow, the publisher, made me cut out *A Pasture of Thorns*... Then I wrote *Ali the Jackal*, which turned out to be called *The Riffian*, published by Atlantic-Little Brown. While Muh Amzzyan, a cripple, stayed at home, ʿAri Ushshan, ʿAli the Jackal, went to France, the Middle Atlas and all over. He was the adventurous half of r-Mnibhi... I wrote this second book with the same combination of organs as in *Flesh*. Nothing I have written ever since compares with these books *because I was a Riffian*' (author's italics).

I can only comment that despite the exaggerations of this final claim, both books are still highly entertaining and, to a very remarkable degree, ethnographically accurate. We now move on in area of action, though remaining in about the same time frame, to two French writers, Piersuis, who wrote about rural Arabic-speaking regions both in the Atlantic coastal plain and around the Wargha River, and René Euloge, one of the finest ethnographers of all, who wrote about the Berber-speaking groups of the Imghran and Imgunn in the high country east of Talwat and above and north of Warzazat and Skura, the area where the Western High Atlas and the Central High Atlas meet. In Piersuis' novels, which we consider first, contacts between local people and Europeans are very noticeably more developed than they are in those of Coon or Euloge.

Piersuis' first novel was *Bourrasque Bédouine* ('Bedouin Squall', Piersuis n.d. but mid-1930s), set in the small (and fictitious) tribal territory of the Zarwala, to whom as of about 1875 Sultan Mawlay al-Hasan I had awarded a tract of land called Maqlukha, in the Hawz or Plain of Marrakesh, as a reward for having furnished a *harka* or military contingent against other, unspecified tribal insurgents. But when the book opens the colonial period is in full swing, and with the establishment of the French protectorate in 1912, some of the Zarwala were no longer on their land but in Marrakesh, and, as they needed money, they sold their title deed to French colons. However, those Zarwala who had stayed at home and whose *ukil* or legal representative Si Tibari, who perishes in a flash flood just as the story begins, had another title deed, one that the local people knew about, that he had kept in his *shkara* or scrip. Bin Hamdun, a local notable, wants to tell the *hakim* or French *contrôleur civil* that the land in question, 50 days' worth of plowing, is their land and that the Zarwali émigrés to Marrakesh had no right to sell it. But the *shaykh* Si Muhammad says he will write him a letter.

Next, Carrel, the Frenchman who is to take over the land in the name of a French agricultural society, is forced to admit that its juridical status is 'not quite clear'. On the spot with his friend Jaminet he only begins to get a vague idea of the complications and pitfalls that will be put in his way by the resident Zarwala, all of whom meet them at the contested area, telling them that they are willing to take the case of their possession to the *qa'id*, to the hakim and to Rabat, and that the individual who sold the title to the company had left Zarwala a century earlier (an obvious exaggeration) and had nothing more to do with it. So Carrel buys a tent and camps on the edge of the property, gradually establishing rapport with some of the villagers by dispensing medicines – and sometimes the *shaykh* even asks him over for lunch. But bin Hamdun, the Zarwali most hostile to him, tells Carrel outright that he will never cultivate the Maqlukha land.

Meanwhile Carrel becomes attracted to a certain Fatima, who turns out to be the widow of Brahim, who was killed in the flood with Si Tibari, and as surreptitiously as possible, she starts to visit him. But she nonetheless appears to be spoken for by bin Hamdun, who wants now either to chase Carrel out of the region or to kill him. The other villagers are more cautious. When Fatima and Carrel go to the *suq* or market, separately, she has her neighbor move her *nwala* or thatch hut closer to his tent. The market is described in fine ethnographic detail and so, earlier, is the sacrifice of a calf at Sidi Bu Darga. In the *suq*, Carrel has a talk with Si Ahsin, Brahim's brother and Fatima's former brother-in-law, and learns that the *Shaykh* Si Muhammad wants to marry her and is really his enemy. He also learns that bin Hamdun is the son of the real owner of a jar of gold coins which the *shaykh* discovered after a camp was pillaged in precolonial times, and as a result of which he gradually became rich. Si Ahsin then wants to sell Carrel the real land deed, according to which the present occupants of Maqlukha are not its real owners. Fatima, now in her *nwala* near Carrel's tent, later tells Carrel that she hates Si Ahsin and that bin Hamdun is the *shaykh*'s son-in-law. Carrel has no intention of giving Si Ahsin 1000 *riyal*-s before he sees the deed about which the latter told him, although Si Ahsin vows privately that he will make Carrel pay more, especially as he is the representative of a company and not a private individual. There follows another good chapter giving an account of a local saint who punishes perjurors at oath, and of stories about *jnun* or malevolent spirits, and how they are exorcised; and Carrel then has another brief confrontation with bin Hamdun, while others prevent them both from coming to blows.

When the hakim and the *qa'id* arrive with paramilitary *mkhazni*-s to measure the limits of the property, there is a general uproar, even though the measurements are taken. Carrel gets sick and is cured by Fatima with paste made from a burnt crow in order to exorcise the *jinn* in his stomach. (The liaison between Carrel and Fatima, which would in any case normally be impossible, is conceived and handled in a very colonialistic and paternalistic fashion, as indeed is Piersuis' very static view of Islam and Muslim civilization. But the descriptive ethnography is very good, and it is quite obvious that the author was at home with Moroccan Arabic.) It is at this point that Si Ahsin presents Fatima with his daughter by her, a daughter named ᶜAisha whom she does not know or recognize, and tells her to take care of the daughter while he goes away: for it seems that he got her pregnant but did not marry her, even though an arrangement was made during her pregnancy whereby, if she lived, she would marry Brahim, Si Ahsin's brother. Then Si Ahsin returns and accuses Fatima of hiding his daughter from him, but she tells him the child is no longer there and has disappeared. Could she possibly have fallen into the well on the property? This is checked, and only the carcass of a goat is pulled out of the well. Bin Hamdun now intervenes to say he will save Fatima if she can persuade Carrel not to cultivate the Maqlukha land; but if not, he will pull the body of ᶜAisha out of the well as proof of what her mother did. And another interlude follows in which the *fqih* Si Ahmida says nostalgically that he would like to return to the days of *siba*, when men were men, and says, furthermore, that the French will eventually have to leave, even against their will...

On his return from Casablanca, where he has gone to see his friend Jaminet, Fatima tells Carrel everything except the fact of having thrown her daughter into the well, sticking to the story that she has simply disappeared. Carrel kicks Fatima out, after which bin Hamdun appears and shoots her. She dies without knowing that Carrel, afterward, has just pardoned her. Bin Hamdun goes to the Jbil l-Kahal to enter a *khalwa*, a retreat, to meditate as a Sufi, and the story ends on a note of Sufi resignation in the face of French, Italian and British colonialism, for it is now the ships of the colonial Christian powers that handle the major part of the *hajj* traffic to and from Jidda (and Mecca).

Piersuis' second novel is *Les Feux du Douar* ('The Fires of the Village', Piersuis 1937), the main theme of which revolves around a modern heresy. The scene is a village called Qmamsha near the Wad Wargha. Here another dispute over another allegedly fraudulent sale of land develops between the village *mqaddim* or headman Zayir Tahar and the *fqih* or schoolmaster Si Jilali, who are both kinsmen and members of a fictitious and very heterodox Sufi order called the Mlushiyin. Enter Carrel once again, who a year after his failure at Maqlukha now has a property on the Wargha, with Jaminet. It transpires that the Mlushiyin are also members of another, hidden order, the Mukhfiya, and as such are exempted from prayer and from fasting during Ramadan. This is admittedly very hard to swallow, but it is crucial to the action of the plot; Piersuis even attempts to tie it in with pre-Islamic Greco-Egyptian cults as well as with early Berber heresies of an anti-Islamic character, about which detailed evidence is in fact very thin.

At any rate, Si Jilali the *fqih* is installed in a small house bordering Carrel's property and they become friends after Carrel sympathizes with Si Jilali's seething resentment of Zayir Tahar, who ejected him from his land and stole it, and whom he cannot regard as a Muslim – and there follows some good commentary on Europeans as seen by Moroccans. Also, even though he hates Zayir Tahar, Si Jilali is very attracted to the latter's daughter ʿAisha.

Zayir Tahar also has a son named Bushta who has become a wandering dervish, who is kicked out of one village but is given new clothes in another. However, he sees a *jinn*, a malevolent spirit, on a windy night, becomes very afraid and has to be calmed down, although later he says it was the Qmamsha saint Sidi Mhammad bin Mumin who chased the *jinn* away.

Zayir Tahar now gets sick and dies, after pardoning his son Bushta, whom he kicked out of the house years earlier; but he dies pronouncing the secret formula of the Mlushiyin and not the *shahada*, the Muslim profession of faith. Si Jilali attends his funeral, after which a quarrel breaks out over his inheritance. Umm l-Khir, his widow, is opposed to the marriage of their daughter to Si Jilali, so the latter tries to enlist the help of an old woman named Batul with a viper's tongue. Batul tries to reason with Umm l-Khir but does not succeed, and they become enemies; while Dmm l-Khir waits for Bushta to come home. But when ʿAisha tells Batul that she is seeing Si Jilali, Umm l-Khir learns of this and beats her daughter. The latter announces that she is leaving, and she goes straight to Si Jilali, who in a bad mood tells her that their liaison is now broken and she should go home. ʿAisha now kills old Batul and dumps her body in a *matmura*, an underground grain storage pit. It is not discovered until long afterward, and nobody cares, as she was very unpopular.

Meanwhile Bushta, who is still on the road, has gone to Fes, where he has an unfortunate experience with a prostitute, but who is not aware that two of the other whores in the house are his sisters Fatthum and Zahra, who escaped from home after Zayir Tahar died. It is only shortly later, after a chance meeting in Fes with a friend from home that he learns of his father's death and decides to return home.

Back in Qmamsha after his long absence, Bushta's *baraka* through his ancestry seems assured, even though he is not very bright, especially as miracles rightly or wrongly attributed to him are spread by word of mouth. Si Jilali, whose vigorously opposing and orthodox views have had some effect on the village, is now once again in a difficult position, especially as his ambition is to build a Friday congregational mosque there. Bushta now flatly forbids ʿAisha to see Si Jilali, and the wealthy Mʿallim Qasim takes his side.

At this point Jaminet, his sister Jeanne and the Abbe Haumont come to see Carrel, who excuses himself from them after Si Jilali comes in to tell him that both the *qa'id* and the *hakim* have threatened him with imprisonment. Carrel's French guests do not take kindly to their host's sudden departure, all of them being self-centered with highly colonialist mentalities (which come through vividly, even though Piersuis was probably quite unaware of them when he wrote). Bushta and the Mʿallim Qasim then plan for the '*nuit de la faute*', the festival of the Mlushiyin, without the presence of Si Jilali; and to this end Bushta returns to Fes to bring back his sisters. He runs into the Abbe in the Armenian canteen without the latter being aware that it is he who has the 'secrets of Berber origins' in his possession, i.e., in the Qmamsha-Mlushiyin documents. But Si Jilali learns of the upcoming 'Night of Error', in which the Mlushiyin do all that is forbidden in Islam. He comes to tell Carrel about it and to say that the *kafir* pigs, led by Bushta, will not permit him to attend, that they will not allow anyone who is not one of them to be present on the night in question. Carrel promises that if he himself sees it he will report on it so that the authorities will forbid it. So they plan to go, in jillabas and with brown skin-darkening fluid rubbed on their legs.

They move on to the *qubba* of Sidi Mansur where the feast is to be held, and from a distance they see Bushta greeting the people arriving, and Si Jilali spots ʿAisha. Bushta sacrifices two sheep, after which the men begin to dance, and the women, all unveiled and all bareheaded, join them. Then the fire-eating begins. Bushta comes out and after an altercation with Si Jilali, the latter throws him into a ravine, while telling his three French friends to flee the scene. This they do, while Jeanne is waiting impatiently for them with the car. The next morning they see a funeral cortege pass by with Si Jilali's body: he had been killed by the crowd at Bushta's order, because on seeing ʿAisha at its edge he refused to leave. So they pulled him to pieces; but he went down fighting righteously, cracking several skulls with his stick and raining the curses of Allah on them for the pigs and impious dogs that they were. So ʿAisha now becomes the second wife of the Mʿallim Qasim, and a child is born to her before nine months have passed. The book ends with the irony that the child, who looks just like its father Si Jilali, will grow up to be a staunch follower of the Mlushiyin heresy. It should, however, be noted that although, and despite its colonialism, all of this may make for an ingenious plot, the heresy itself as posited here is almost a millennium too late, for the last recorded one in Morocco occurred before 1200 CE.

A third work by Piersuis worth considering here is *L'Oeil de Mahmoud* ('Mahmud's Eye', Piersuis 1947), a series of twelve essentially unrelated short stories, all using various incidents in or aspects of Moroccan history as points of reference and all arranged chronologically. They have only one connecting thread, which is genetic in character: the appearance in most of them of someone with mismatched or misproportioned eyes, in whom the right eye is situated higher than the left one. A few examples will suffice: In the first, 'Pour l'Amour de Tiski' ('For the Love of Tiski'), Yazid, a lieutenant of ʿUqba bin Nafiʿ, generally recognized as the first Arab conqueror of North Africa, finally marries a Berber girl named Tiski after escaping from ʿUqba's followers; and the child born of the union, Muhand wuld l-ʿArbi ('Son of the Arab') has his right eye located higher than his left. This is here interpreted to mean that the eye of the Arab will dominate that of the Berber; and so the child grows up to become one of the servitors of Mawlay Idris the Younger (803-828 CE), the founder of Fes.

In the fourth story, 'Les Têtes Coupées' ('The Severed Heads'), a very much later sultan, Mawlay Ismaʿil (1672-1727), well known for his extreme severity to tribal rebels, orders his chamberlain and the latter's assistants to take a mound of exactly 716 severed heads from a battlefield in the Tadla region on the western edge of the Atlas back to Fes to adorn the gates. He tells them that if they lose any along the way, their own heads will be forfeit as a result, in order to fill the quota. With a large mule train loaded with heads (23 mules with 30 heads apiece, and a final one with 26), during the course of fording rivers and stumbling over mountains, a good many heads are indeed lost, but the ingenuity that the chamberlain and the mule drivers show in order to make up the remainder (through robbing graveyards, etc.) is the core of the story. Finally, the number of 715, including one female skull, is reached, and for the final one the halves of two different skulls taken from a cemetery are glued together; and once again, the right eye socket is higher than the left.

In the eighth, 'Les Oreilles de Moha' ('Muha's Ears'), a Susi goatherd named Muha wuld ʿAqqa of the Id aw-Tanan tribe, who has both mismatched eyes and enormous ears, goes north to the Ulad ʿAmran of the Dukkala confederacy during the reign of Mawlay Sulayman (1792-1822). In the course of a minor local tax-collecting expedition the *qa'id* of the Ahmar and Dukkala tribes tries to force him into paying one *riyal* as tax on his tent. But as a stranger he refuses to pay, and says he would surrender his ears before doing so. He goes further north, but later returns and is trapped by the *qa'id*, who duly has his ears cut off. In the next scene, a robber known simply as l-Hawzi now goes north to the Maʿmura Forest and the Zimmur-Bni Hsin region, and makes off with a Zimmuri flock after beating and tying up the shepherd and his Jewish 'brother'. But he is unaware of the *tata* relationship (which is well described) of cross-tribal sponsorship between individuals and lineage groups of both tribes, and hence does not know that the Jew is an *u-tata* with both a Hasnawi (Bni Hsin) and a Zimmuri of the Mzurfa section. The sheep he has stolen from the Zimmur are valued by the *qa'id* at 5 rifles and 5 daggers, plus 100 *riyal*-s as indemnity to be given to the Jew. The Zimmuri *qa'id* says he will cut off the Hawzi's ears, as happened in another recently famous case, if he does not accept these conditions. But he does accept, and then takes off his turban to show that his ears are already missing, saying that if he has lost them for only 1 1/4 *riyal*-s, he has gained them again, figuratively, through obtaining over one hundred sheep. His astuteness wins the approbation of the camp, and the following week the Zimmur go back to their old sport of pillaging the Saturday market of the Bni Hsin.

The ninth story, 'La Légende de la Pierre Hantée ('The Legend of the Haunted Rock') deals with the relationship between men and *jnun* (pl. of *jinn*); and even Si Birrwʿayn, gifted *fqih* though he is, with his right eye higher than his left, finally succumbs to the *jnun* in the cave where he is looking for buried treasure. And in the final story, 'L'Aventure de Mme. Ragle' ('The Adventure of Mme. Ragle'), the misproportioned eyes appear once again in a three-year old boy, nicknamed Mahmud, who is befriended and adopted by a Frenchwoman, Mme. Ragle, but whose real name is Muhammad bin ʿAbdallah, the same name as that of the Prophet.

René Euloge must be classed, along with Carleton Coon, as one of the finest names in ethnographic fiction from any part of North Africa and the Middle East at large during the colonial period. As Coon was largely though not entirely bound by the Rif, in Euloge's case the region dealt with was circumscribed to Demnat, the upper Tasawt valley and the high peaks where the

Western Atlas joins the Central Atlas. This is to say, the region between the Iglawn (Ar. Glawa) of Talwat and the Tizi n-Tishka pass and the Ait ᶜAtta of Usikis-Msimrir (who fell outside his purview, but directly into my own: cf. Hart 1981), the region east of Demnat and north of Warzazat, Skura and l-Qalᶜa Mguna, encompassing the various tribal groups, all very composite in make-up and structure, of the Inultan (Ultana), the Infdwak (Ftwaka), the Ait ᶜAbbas, the Imghran and the Imgunn (Mguna). About these particular Berber tribes Euloge wrote with a firm and sure ethnographic hand; it is not often that he can be caught out in an outright error. His stories, most of them carefully dated, go back to the late 1920s and early 1930s, before the French 'pacification' of the Atlas was fully achieved, and are thus more or less contemporaneous with Coon's novels on the Rif. The publication, or republication of most of them was delayed until the early 1950s, and in the case of one somewhat overlapping collection, until 1976. But they all combine an intimate knowledge of the region and its people with a superb eye for the important features of the ethnography as well as a driving sense of narrative; and they are among the very best of their kind.

We begin with two long short stories, or novelettes, in a volume entitled *Silhouettes du Pays Chleuh* ('Silhouettes of a Berber Region', Euloge 1951), which may well be, as noted, be a republication of a 1931 original, as it has a preface by Maurice Le Glay, whose own output was not at all in the same class with that of Euloge. In the first story, 'La Chkara' ('The Scrip', dated 1930, with the title referring to Moroccan Arabic *shkara*, a decorated leather shoulder bag in which Moroccan men formerly carried their valuables), the action takes place at the beginning of the reign of the sultan Mawlay Yusuf (1912-27), i.e., at the beginning of the French protectorate but before its effective implantation in the region under discussion. It is, in fact, a Berber version of a detective story, although for the reader the identity of the murderer is no secret. A certain Si Brahim w-ᶜAli n-Ait Baddu is the *nazir* of *habus* property (religious endowments, usually in land, made over to mosques by pious individuals, and more apt to be found in urban contexts than in rural ones) in the small town of Demnat. Much respected locally, he is nonetheless heavily in debt because most of his wealth has been squandered on easy living. An emissary from the vizirate of *habus* comes to tell him that if within three months he has not paid up the 6,000 duros hasani that he has owed them for over a year, he will be stripped of his job and jailed. He thinks of and then rejects various ways to raise the money, and then he recalls an offer already made two or three times for the Ait Baddu property just outside Demnat by old Si Muhammad n-Ait Ukhkham, known as Baba ᶜAgirba or 'Father Scorpion', a former *amin al-binnaya* or head of the qasba-builders' guild, who has neither family nor heirs. (This man once discovered a sum of money hidden in a deserted qasba, and hence his nickname, as only scorpions live in such places, and hence also his reputation as a diviner.) Baba ʿAgirba agrees to buy the Ait Baddu property for 20,000 duros hasani, even though the land is unirrigated.

But Si Brahim starts to ponder something else that Baba ʿAgirba has said, that he would come to his house in the qasba on the following Thursday with the money, and would not return to Demnat any more until he got rich because people there have been persecuting him. Then Si Brahim sends Baba ʿAgirba a note saying that he will meet him at the now dilapidated Ait Baddu property. On his way to the meeting Baba ʿAgirba is then cajoled into buying a new yellow *shkara*, a new bag or scrip, from the merchant l-ʿArbi sh-Shka'iri in Demnat, even while still carrying his old one filled with money to pay Si Brahim. The latter is extremely bitter about having to sell up but he hides it well in front of Baba ʿAgirba, now about to become Sidi Muhammad n-Ait Ukhkham; and Baba ʿAgirba's continual niggling about repairs needed for old roof-beams and the like has made Si Brahim decide to kill him before his departure. The die is cast when Baba ʿAgirba says he will not give Si Brahim a *muzuna* (a very small coin) before the deed of sale has been correctly drawn up by the ʿ*adl* or notary Si Qasim. So Si Brahim waits for just the right moment to come behind Baba ʿAgirba and stab him vigorously in the neck. Indeed, he does so with such force as almost to detach Baba ʿAgirba's head from his body, which he pushes into a cistern storing irrigation water. He manages to get both *shkara*-s back from the body, which he wraps in its owner's burnous, although his dagger blade is solidly embedded in the corpse and he cannot retrieve it.

Si Brahim has of course made sure that there were no witnesses to the murder, but now he will never sell nor rent his property, so he goes to tell his old servant ʿAbdilbi (ʿAbd an-Nabi) never to let anyone in. Then he returns to his house in Demnat to count Baba ʿAgirba's money. Old ʿAbdilbi dies while Si Brahim is on his way to Marrakesh to pay his debts. Twice during his absence an old man in a green turban calls to see him, but Tahamu, his old nurse, tells him on his return that it was not Baba ʿAgirba and that the man did not give his name. Nonetheless, Si Brahim has agonizing thoughts. And Si ʿAbbas, the *bu mwarit* or administrator of estates in abeyance who has told Si Brahim of ʿAbdilbi's death, now discovers that Si Brahim is carrying a new dagger.

The old man in the green turban returns, also wearing a yellow *shkara*, and proves to be an emissary of the *Qa'id* Ushttu of Tanant, who says he will pay

50,000 duros for the Ait Baddu property. The sight of the *shkara* makes Si Brahim go back in secret to Ait Baddu to see if he got rid of Baba ʿAgirba's old *shkara* after removing all the latter's money, papers and other contents. But the old *shkara* is not there, and he then chases out a little girl who has been cutting grass after she casually mentions Baba ʿAgirba's name. He learns subsequently from the bu mwarit, however, that old ʿAbdilbi has an heir, Lahsin, the owner of the tea-shop in the village of Ait Umghar. It turns out that this heir has the *shkara* in question, which Si Brahim says the bu mwarit has asked him to look for. But when he burns the parcel after getting home, it turns out to be a very old and worn *shkara* which belonged to ʿAbdilbi in any case.

So Si Brahim's worries begin again. He feels no remorse over the murder, but is nonetheless terrified of being discovered; and not being content with what Euloge refers to as the usual Arab *maktub*-type attitude of 'it is written', he wants, naturally enough, to take every possible precaution that he can. The thought of the missing *shkara* has even taken away his taste for women. But his old nurse Tahamu suggests that he should marry the daughter of the *qadi* Si Hmad Iqban who was widowed only a year earlier. While at the barber's, Si Brahim learns that Si l-ʿArbi sh-Shka'iri, the *shkara* maker, has become rich through inheritance from an uncle, as predicted to him by Baba ʿAgirba, who is now believed by all and sundry to have disappeared or died.

Si Hasan Aghujdam, the *shaykh* of Tisart, wants to return the nice yellow *shkara* embroidered with blue silk to the *nazir* Si Brahim, who probably left it with his old servitor. His son Si ʿAli takes it to an outdoor *nzaha* feast during the month before Ramadan where it is recognized by Si l-ʿArbi sh-Shka'iri as the one he gave Baba ʿAgirba just after he has announced that he wants to sacrifice a bull at the shrine of Mawlay ʿAbd al-Qadir al-Jilali in memory of Baba ʿAgirba for his good fortune. So Si l-ʿArbi sh-Shka'iri suddenly jumps on Si ʿAli because he thinks the latter may have killed Baba ʿAgirba. Si ʿAli then explains how his father found the *shkara* in the room in the qasba where ʿAbdilbi lived, thinking it more likely that it belonged to his master. Then Si Brahim, also invited to the nzaha, and after greetings, sees the *shkara* and immediately and abruptly takes off. Si Hasan Aghujdam arrives just after his departure and Lahsin the tea-house owner announces that Si Brahim was the well-dressed man who took the *shkara* from him to return to the bu mwarit. Si Hasan then tells the others not to say a word about this.

Meanwhile Si Brahim rushes back to Ait Baddu to see that the cistern into which he dumped Baba ʿAgirba's body is properly covered up; but the next day a girl he knows scares him by mentioning Baba ʿAgirba's name again. Later he learns from his barber that Lahsin the tea-house owner has been arrested on suspicion of having murdered Baba ʿAgirba and of leaving the latter's *shkara* with his late uncle ʿAbdilbi. Then the qadi urges Si Brahim to empty the cistern at Ait Baddu because everyone at Tisart will need the irrigation water when their mown runs out.

After this old Tahamu dies and the *qadi* announces that after he has come back from his next trip to Marrakesh, Si Brahim's marriage to his daughter will take place. Later, in conversation, at an *ahwash* dance, the *shaykh* of Tisart, his son, the bu mwarit and the *qadi* are all determined to obtain Si Brahim's views on the disappearance of Baba ʿAgirba, whose *shkara*, the *khalifa* Si Bu Krim says, was found at his place or at his servant's. The *khalifa* thinks that Baba ʿAgirba may well have been attacked and killed by bandits, as has happened to a number of people in the region, but he also thinks that he had to pass through Ait Baddu. It is then that the yellow *shkara* is shown to Si Brahim by the *khalifa*. Si Brahim almost strangles in his throat but the *khalifa* eases the situation for him slightly by saying that they are all among friends, that Baba ʿAgirba was no friend to any of them, and that he may well have been killed by the late ʿAbdilbi in an old men's quarrel. But then Si Brahim falls into a trap when he says that Lahsin the tea-house owner as well as he himself would say that ʿAbdilbi would never have had a *shkara* as luxurious as this one. The session is then broken up when a runner, a *raqqas*, comes in to announce the death of the Qa'id ʿAbd al-Malik bin Si Madani al-Glawi (in 1916) in battle at Bu Yihya at the hands of the 'dissident' Ait Massad tribe.

The *khalifa*, the bu mwarit and the *shaykh* are all convinced now of Si Brahim's guilt but they also agree that he has been 'saved' by the death of Qa'id ʿAbd al-Malik. But a week or so after they decide to abandon their inquiry, they suddenly see a crazy man jump out and cry, '*Baba ʿAgirba! Baba ʿAgirba! Sh-shkara! Sh-shkara!*' And thus they see God's punishment of the nazir Si Brahim, when the qasba of Ait Baddu falls into ruins.

In this excellent suspense story, Euloge leaves us in no doubt about Si Brahim's motivations behind his murder of Baba ʿAgirba, and also about the fact that he feels no remorse but is, even so, haunted in his dreams and terrified of being caught, especially through some slip-up on his own part. This proves implicitly to have been the case at the end. Whether the crazy man who jumps out from behind a bush to scream '*Baba ʿAgirba! Sh-shkara!*' represents what fear has reduced Si Brahim to is not expressly stated, but it seems safe to assume that this is so and that it is divine retribution and the burden that Si Brahim must forever bear. The deductive or detective work done by Si Bu Krim the *khalifa*, Si ʿAbbas the bu mwarit and Si Hasan the *shaykh*, in tandem, so to speak, is also admirably portrayed, as is their baiting of Si Brahim, a member of their peer group in the basically Berber-speaking but also bilingual society of Demnat (where Arabic *ma n'arif*, 'I don't know', also equals Berber *ur sinagh*), where Arabophone Zimranis impinge upon Berberophone Ghujdamis, Ntifis or Ftwakis. What is also admirable about Euloge's stories is, as we shall continue to see, that all the characters are Moroccans (unlike those of Piersuis), Berbers for the most part, Arabs only occasionally; but except for local hearsay, he keeps the French 'protectors' very largely out. This point may of course be criticized, but given the period that Euloge was writing about, I feel that he was thoroughly justified in maintaining this exclusion.

The second story in *Silhouettes du Pays Chleuh* is 'Marjana' (undated), set in terms of time at an early stage in the French 'pacification' of the West Central Atlas, somewhat prior to 1920. It opens at the French encampment of Asdramt near the Asif n-Birnat, which is under siege by some 600 tribesmen of the Ait Massad. A young girl named Mina Si Hasi n-Ait Tainit has suddenly appeared in the camp to put herself under French protection, and to tell the French officer-in-charge her reasons for doing so. These follow herewith.

The locale now shifts to the Qasba Aghulid in the Gattiwa (or Gattaya) country, inhabited by Si Hasi n-Ait Tainit and his only daughter Mina. Her three brothers are all dead, one drowned in a flood and the other two killed by the Ait Massad. Si Hasi's children were born to a now deceased wife and since then he has married, successively, four more women, all subsequently divorced on grounds of barrenness, and he is bitter about no longer having a male heir. He gives his daughter a *sunduq* or box with all her mother's jewelry as well as the Ait Tainit property deeds and tells her that a great friend will soon visit him whose name he cannot yet reveal. She wonders aloud to their old servant Tawnza if this man might not be the brigand known as 'the Inteketto'. She hopes at least that he is not her younger uncle Bil-Gasim, with whom her father quarreled but about whom he refuses to divulge further information. Her father now engages a *tafqirt*, an older woman, for her as a companion, Lalla Mrisha from the Zawiya Tanaghmalt, who is effusive but insincere and cunning and whom she instinctively dislikes. Mina's cousin Tuda arrives and says that Mrisha is none other than Batul n-Ait Minzil, a sorceress and Bil-Gasim's concubine, and they quarrel immediately. Tuda says Si Hasi has been bewitched by Mrisha, and Mina wants to hear from her all about her uncle Bil-Gasim and 'the Inteketto', to whom Tuda refers as Sidi Fars, because she has been virtually forbidden to mention their names. She knows that Bil-Gasim, also a widower, has had a profligate life, and that he became estranged from his straight-laced brother, her father, because of his marriage to a *shaykha*, a dancing girl from Marrakesh. He also managed to get many local women into his bed, thereby earning the hostility of numerous people in the region. But she learns that Bil-Gasim also has a son. Tuda tells Si Hasi that he must get Mina married and also that he must get rid of Mrisha or Batul. To Si Hasi it seems that the only possible marriage choice for his daughter is her patriparallel cousin, his brother's son.

At this point Si Hasi's old milk brother Mulid appears and then dies of food poisoning. Mina and Mrisha are attacked by robbers on the way to Sidi Baghi, but they are saved by the Inteketto bandit, who escorts them back to Aghulid. Once the Inteketto has taken them home, however, Mrisha claims that the robbers were his own men; and this makes Mina more suspicious of her than ever.

And now according to a messenger, illness has struck at Ait Minzil, the property of Si Hasi's brother Bil-Gasim, who he says has had a stroke and says he wants to see his brother before he dies. However, this is apparently just a ruse, for Si Hasi on the way meets a shepherd who tells him that, to the contrary, Bil-Gasim is in excellent health. His servant Idir then tells him how much his brother Bil-Gasim really hates him, because he will not support him any longer, and Bil-Gasim's daughter Ta'zizit (by the *shaykha* from Marrakesh) has had to turn prostitute in order to make money for him.

That night Mina notes that Mrisha has stolen the key to her father's coffer where his wife's jewelry and all his papers are kept, and tells him so. He catches Mrisha red-handed and kicks her out of the house at last, to everyone's relief. But now he insists that Mina must marry her patricousin Bassu u-bil-Gasim in order to save the Ait Tainit lineage, as Bassu is its last male member just as Mina is its last female.

Then Si Hasi dies. The *fqih* Mulay ʿAli now tells Mina that it is her father's last wish that she go to live with her uncle Bil-Gasim at Ait Minzil and celebrate her marriage with his son Bassu, as soon as the latter recovers from an illness. At this point Bil-Gasim himself suddenly appears, after his brother's funeral, knowing that he and his son will now become wealthy. The *fqih* now tells Mina the story of Shanfura, a very ugly individual in pre-Islamic times who was insulted by the men of another tribe, so he swore to kill one hundred of them. He killed 99 and then died. At his death his enemies mocked him; and ten years later the son of one of them kicked his skull and died from a very slight wound the next day – so he got his full quota of one hundred victims at last.

Once they arrive at Ait Minzil, Mina and Tuda have the qasba gate opened to them by Taʿzizit, who is a girl of Mina's age, and by a very dark, thin near-Hartaniya or black girl from southern Morocco named Marjana. She is taken by them to meet Bil-Gasim, whom Tuda does not greet before leaving. The *fqih* Mulay ʿAli comes to Ait Minzil to tell Mina just how Bassu u-bil-Gasim got sick: the Inteketto bandit ambushed and robbed him in a gorge as he was returning from the market, insulted him, took his clothes and flung him into the cold water of the river. Bassu now returns from a visit to a saint's shrine, still rather sick, and Mina says that she recognizes him as one of her attackers at Sidi Baghi, which he denies. But he is called *Dib* (Ar., 'jackal') by someone, the same nickname that one of her attackers had. She swears to bil-Gasim that his son maltreated her earlier at Sidi Baghi and that she would not have known what to do if the Inteketto had not arrived. Bil-Gasim threatens to shut her up in a silo in solitary confinement, and she now avoids him and Bassu as much as possible. The latter says that she will be his wife whether she wants to be or not. At this point the little black girl Marjana, undernourished and sick, dies on the way back from the spring with a jug of water, which breaks as she falls.

The *fqih* Mulay ʿAli now comes again to Ait Minzil with an ʿadl or notary to see that Mina's interests in her late father's property are upheld. Bil-Gasim, angered, throws them out of the house. Mulay ʿAli swears he will come back to get Mina away from bil-Gasim, who along with his son has greatly dishonored his brother's memory. He says he will also report him to the *Qa'id* Ushttu, his superior, who is interested in the Ait Tainit property, for Mina is now terrified. She overhears Mrisha discussing recipes for *suhur*, sorcery, with another woman, and says she will tell bil-Gasim on her. But bil-Gasim and Mrisha are friends, of course, and bil-Gasim wants them to go together to the market in Demnat the next day.

Mulay ʿAli would like to marry Mina himself but does not want to go against her father's dying wish that she marry Bassu u-bil-Gasim. Or so he is thinking on his way home on his mule, when he is suddenly ambushed, robbed and killed. On hearing this bad news, which means that there is now no obstacle in bil-Gasim's way as far as his brother's inheritance is concerned, Tuda decides to return to Ait Minzil, only to find that bil-Gasim is about to send Mina, who is suffering from headaches, to Sidi Bu Ghalf with two rams for sacrifice, and under the surveillance of Bassu and Mrisha, who grab Mina and tie her up so that Tuda cannot hear her. She insults Bassu about his encounter with the Inteketto, so he breaks a water-jug over her head on hearing the latter's name pronounced. At this point bil-Gasim announces that Mina will now take the place and the name of Marjana, the dead Drawiya servant girl; and her thralldom now begins in earnest.

At this point, however, news comes that the Irumiyen, the Christians, have arrived and are camping at Tanant, on their way up to Azilal. *Qa'id* Ushttu has submitted to them, as has *Qa'id* Bziwi; but the *igurramen* or saints of the Zawiya Ahansal have raised up all the Central Atlas in revolt from the Ait Mhand to the Ait Is'hha, and there is more fighting every day. The Inteketto, meanwhile, appears to have rallied to the invaders and is engaging in *harka* warfare on their behalf from the Ait Attab to the Ait Bu Iknifen, or Ait ᶜAtta (presumably those of Talmast, possibly also those of Usikis-Msimrir, but this is not specified). During all this time Mina must still do all the donkey work while answering to countless insults as well as to the name of the little black girl Marjana, shouted at her in scorn.

But she knows that the Inteketto is not far away and wants desperately to escape from Ait Minzil and seek his protection. She finds an opportunity to do so when Mrisha sends her out to fetch water; and she wanders into the Inteketto's camp to give herself to him in exchange for his protection. She even learns to shoot a musket in his company and finds that she enjoys inflicting punishment on captives. But bil-Gasim meanwhile discovers that she is now with the Inteketto so he gets together a sixty-man *harka* in order to kill the latter and to bring Mina back to marry his son Bassu so as to rid himself of *Qa'id* Ushttu's importunings. And in a pitched battle with this force, just after telling Mina in which direction to escape, the Inteketto is killed.

Mina is then recaptured and taken back to Ait Minzil by bil-Gasim's people. She finds on arrival there that people are no longer calling her 'Marjana', that Taᶜzizit has escaped to a whorehouse in Demnat and that Tuda has married a camel driver from the Bni Miskin (which seems odd, as the Bni Miskin are not mountain Berbers at all, but flatland Arabs, and possibly as poor as their name would suggest). Bassu is still sick, but the marriage now takes place, with Mina sick at heart. She is tied up for three days while bil-Gasim says that Bassu will take a second wife to whom she will be a servant. Mrisha covers her stomach with thuya tar and Bassu spits in her face when she tells him that he will never be able to make love to her as the Inteketto did.

This completes her recital to the French commandant in the bivouac as Asdramt. She escapes at night after having thought to have been killed by rifle fire outside the camp. Later, near Ait Tagilla, two *mkhazni*-s are spotted escorting back to Azilal a woman who admits to having just poisoned her father-in-law and her husband, who was her parallel cousin, with arsenic bought from an ambulant vendor; but she is consumed with fever and dies on the road.

In his preface to this story, dated July 1938, Georges Louis remarked that it is a very Berber variation on the theme of the heart versus the social order, a conflict which in this case exists mainly because of the abominable character of the dissolute Bassu and his father bil-Gasim, who is also held to have been a murderer several times over, a point hinted at but not completely clarified by Euloge. Otherwise Mina would willingly have listened to and obeyed her dying father's decrees and Berber custom would have resolved the problems created by love vs. tribal life.

In his next collection of short stories, *Les Derniers Fils de l'Ombre* ('The Last Sons of the Shade', Euloge 1952), it is not without interest to note that in an introductory essay written originally in 1928-1929 and entitled 'Des Horizons d'Hier a Demain' ('From the Horizons of Yesterday to Those of Tomorrow'), Euloge, even before the promulgation by the French of the 'Berber Dahir' or decree of 1930 (by which, as noted earlier, Berber-speaking tribes in the French zone of Morocco were removed from Shariᶜa legal jurisdiction, that of Islamic law, and were placed instead into that of Berber *izirf* or *qaᶜida*, customary law, an act which caused a furor all over the Muslim world: cf. Hart 1997[b]), shows himself, by implication, to have been very much against it. For he says: 'it would be a profound error to think that one could set against the Arab conqueror the Berber autochthone by giving him a European education which would turn him against the Koran and would attempt to make an anti-Islamic force of him. The force of Islam lies precisely in the strict and unbreakable communion of all believers whatever their nationalities, and if Berbers and Arabs are of different races, languages and customs, they are brothers in religion: *the indissoluble tie that links them together under all circumstances is Islam* (author's italics). How many quarrels that might have degenerated into violence between Berbers and Arabs have been halted by the voice of a single man asking, '*Ntuma Msilmin u la*? Are you Muslims or not?' (ibid.: 14). Still another quote from the same essay, but of a different kind, that I cannot resist is that in the late 1920s in the upper Uzighim and Imdghas valleys in the Atlas Euloge was sometimes even asked by Berber tribesmen, '*Illa kra ugillid*? Is it true that there is a sultan?' (ibid.: 16).

In the first story in this collection, 'La Nzala du Tidili' ('The *Nzala* of Tidili', 1926), on a winter day at the teahouse of Qahwaji ᶜAbbas there arrives Si Bu ᶜAziz, a wealthy landowner, and a couple of men accompanying him, as well as his two wives and a daughter just married to the son of a *qa'id*. Inside the teahouse is a wild-looking man named Zabul who is regarded as good-for-nothing but who is an expert at slaughtering animals. He touches lovingly the flintlock gun of Si Bu ᶜAziz, who tells him peremptorily to put it down, and identifies it as a *bushfar* from Tiznit. Si Bu ᶜAziz says it belonged to a bandit named Talkut who had a duro encrusted into the barrel for each man he killed; and he then says it was he himself who captured Talkut twenty years earlier. So the rest of them beg him to explain how this happened, and with some reluctance, and bit by bit, he does so — while Zabul makes occasional unsolicited comments. Indeed, at one point Zabul accuses Si Bu ᶜAziz of lying, when he says he was able to hold off the bandit who was just about to shoot him, for *Qa'id* Najim had put a price on Talkut's head. Zabul adds that this price was 5,000 duros hasani; and they wonder how Si Bu ᶜAziz would otherwise have acquired his olive grove in Tidili and his qasba at Ait Talib. Zabul has also been 'reading' the fortunes of ᶜAbbas' guests in a pile of small stones, out of which he now also begins to 'read' the story of Talkut, whose father was swindled out of his property by a neighbor, the *Qa'id* Smaᶜin, and went to an early grave. Talkut took to the hills as a bandit and the 5,000 duro price was put on his head, and in one battle he alone escaped when all his men were killed. He was badly wounded, however, and took refuge, Zabul says, with a man who wanted to strangle him in his sleep. Instead of doing so, however, he went to look for the *qa'id*'s *mkhazni*-s to finish him off. After a number of men fielded both by Sultan Mawlay al-Hasan I (1873-1894) and by his vizier Ba Ahmad (1894-1900), who took over the reins of state during an interregnum after his death, had been killed during their passage through the upper Tasawt valley, Talkut's head was taken back to adorn the walls of Marrakesh. Zabul says he was six years old when the executioner beheaded Talkut. But the real curses were reserved for the men who had betrayed the laws of hospitality by turning Talkut over to the *mkhazni*-s of the *Qa'id* Najim, who was himself killed twelve years later, as was the executioner Salah Wultani, and everyone else who had had a hand in Talkut's demise. Then Zabul asks Si Bu ᶜAziz why he now seems to possess Talkut's flintlock; and after this he throws his stones on the fire and leaves. But the simple Zabul is in fact none other than Talkut's son; and he comes back later to kill Si Bu ᶜAziz, to reclaim his father's *bushfar* and Si Bu ᶜAziz' married daughter whom he seizes to take with him and to give Talkut grandchildren.

The next story, 'La Vallée d'Anefgou' (The Valley of Anfgu, 1923), begins with an opening quotation which is amply borne out by the story itself:

> *'Ala baba innek, iwi, inghit amghar / Aw talat, mma, lamghar amghdar zund shitan immut / Mayi-t-ighan? / L-hasift!*
> 'Weep for your father, my son, the *amghar* has killed him! Don't cry, mother, the treacherous and diabolical *amghar* is dead! Who killed him? Vengeance!'

In the Anfgu valley, probably located in the Western Atlas not far from the Seksawa country (although there is another of the same name in the Ait Hadiddu territory of the Southeastern Atlas), there are two settlements, Ait Ibuqaden and Ait Idarfan, which face each other across the river; and the alluvial land between them has been carefully plotted out for irrigation. But one day the *Amghar* Udardur ('Deaf'), who is what Euloge calls a *shaykh s-siba*, a local strongman rather than an elected chief and who has the *aitarbi'in*, the council, totally in his pocket, thinks he sees a way to take over this rich alluvial land by the river, where he now only has four small plots; and he prays that the Almighty will aid him in his plan. A week later he asks Mbark, the guardian of the division of irrigation water, if he has carried out his orders, and the latter replies that for eight days now he has cut off the water as much to the detriment of the Ibuqaden as to that of the Idarfan, that nobody has any idea that it is the guardian himself and the *amghar*'s two nephews who are playing with the *uggug*, the ditch head. The local irrigators should indeed watch out, because while one man draws them upstream by his cries, the other cuts the *targa*, the irrigation ditch itself, downstream, and two men have already come to blows. The guardian himself has feigned indignation and has threatened to leave the region, so he tells the *amghar*.

Things are looking well for *Amghar* Udardur, who resolves to get rid of the guardian Mbark permanently once his usefulness is over, either through a bowl of poisoned milk or by having him pushed off the roof of a qasba. He also gives conflicting advice to the *inflas*, the notables, of both the Ibuqaden and the Idarfan, both of whom then assemble at night and begin to quarrel in earnest, when two shots ring out and a man of each side falls, shot down by the *amghar*'s two nephews, Salim and Fars, who are both good marksmen.

So a battle now breaks out full tilt. In due course Udardur appears with his men to tell both sides that they are crazy and that the only way to resolve the conflict – after five men are dead and twenty wounded – is to place the entire valley and its fields under his control until such time as good relations between the two lineage groups can resume. But mutual hatred between them impedes any reconciliation, with none of the inhabitants of one village visiting the saint's shrine of the other or taking the same path to the *suq* – and what happens is that they both become the *ikhammasen*, the sharecroppers, of *Amghar* Udardur. Ten whole years pass in this way, and then Mbark suddenly takes sick. Before dying he confesses to the *inflas*, the notables of both lineage groups that it was the *amghar* who audaciously planned the whole maneuver. So they intercept *Amghar* Udardur as he is saddling up his mule and he dies on the spot as the result of no less than eighteen stab wounds.

In 'La Nuit du Destin' ('The Night of Destiny', 1928), there is a conflict in the village of Ait Umghar east of Demnat, between Si Nasir n-Ait Umghar and the Hajj Jilali, the master of Demnat, who has taken over the former's land. Si Nasir is sick and on the Night of Destiny, 27 Ramadan, he has delusions which nonetheless prove real. He stabs Hajj Jilali and is in turn killed by the latter's black slave, thus escaping the effects of a poisoned kuskus prepared for him by a *tasahhart*, a sorceress. This story, in our view, is definitely not one of Euloge's best, not at all in a class with the superlative one about the Anfgu valley, above.

'Le Rempart des Morts' ('The Ramparts of the Dead', 1929) begins with another Berber proverb: *l-uqt-ad, tamazirt-nnagh ghir l-khuf u l-mut*, 'In those days in our country there was only fear and death' (ibid.: 81). Muhammad u-Ya$^c$qub, the *shaykh* of the Ait Iggut in the Sirwa region, builds a large *agadir* or collective storehouse during the *siba* or precolonial period; and it is later discovered that two of his best workers, a pair of homosexuals, murdered some sixty of the others for all they could get from them. The next season the Znaga warriors overrun the weakened Ait Iggut where the skeletons of the murdered workers have been found in all the walls. Hence the name *sur l-miyyitin*, the ramparts of the dead.

'Le Bon Temps' ('The Good Old Days', 1927) provides us with yet another opening proverb: *Iksud yaghuld argaz iwggar am mush*, 'Fear renders a man more cruel than a cat' (ibid.: 93). This one is the story of a bandit raid on a mule caravan at Tasimsit in the Infdwak (Ftwaka), where the locals had a very bad reputation as bandits; while fear of the redoubtable *amghar* of the Ait l-Hajj $^c$Ali made them kill and throw the bodies of the last survivors, including that of a girl, into a cave.

In 'Fin de Dissidence' ('The End of Dissidence', 1925), the difficult decision of whether to surrender to the French or to keep on fighting is posed to *Amghar* Haddu of the Ait Azinqud, in a region which has always previously had a spotless resistance record. The tale is told of a local girl who, after a French lieutenant was killed, cut off his testicles, then opened up his stomach and filled it with stones. This comes up while the *amghar* is making a nose-count of who has already been killed and who is still alive. The living are in the minority, and tales are now told that the French have not destroyed mosques as was feared, and that they have set up medical centers. But the *amghar* himself, although he advises his people to opt for *l-aman*, surrender, will not do so, for *ur llin sin dyuk g-l-ʿash n-igidar*, 'there cannot be two males in the eagle's nest' (ibid.: 105). So he dies in battle, in a calculated replay of the last days of Muha u-Hammu Amhazun Aziyyi, the famous top *qa'id* of the Iziyyan.

In 'Soumission' ('Submission', 1928), which takes place in Imghran territory, Bassu n-Ait u-Qantul, who hunts snakes in order to extract their poison, is returning one night to his village of Asaka when he is almost captured by a sixty-man *harka*, a war party under the *khalifa* Si Bu Rahhal, who, with the Ait Zaghrar, is heading up to force the Ait u-Qantul to submit to the authority of the Glawi. They are just about ready to attack them when Bassu calls out loudly to warn the *amghar*, Muhammad Asardu, that the Glawi's *khalifa* has surrounded Asaka. But he is quickly silenced by a blow on the head. A man comes out of the main gate of the *qsar* to denounce the *khalifa* and his total force of 200 men of the Ait Zaghrar and other Imghran sections as cowards for not having fired the two warning shots, or *timatarin*, that traditionally preceded a battle between rival Berber groups. But the *khalifa* addresses *Amghar* Asardu gravely and assures him of the protection of the *qa'id* of Talwat and of the French. Nonetheless, the *amghar* fires on him, and the *khalifa* returns the fire, breaking both the *amghar's* legs above the knee. The village still refuses to surrender, so the attack and the resulting pillage by the *khalifa's* men begin. Not a single house escapes it, and as many of the village's inhabitants as can do so flee.

But there are no dead and the *amghar* himself is the only casualty. The *khalifa* tells the Ait u-Qantul that they must accept the tutelage of Si Hammu l-Glawi, and then says that he will only confiscate the village's sheep as *fard*, the obligatory collective payment, and not its mules, cattle or goats, nor will he impose fines on any of its members. One old man tries to convince the *khalifa* that his daughter has been raped, but when she points out no less than six men whom she regards as possibly or probably responsible for the deed, the *khalifa* sends them packing. He demands the loyalty of the Ait u-Qantul to the Glawi and they finally declare it, swearing fidelity to him and claiming his protection. And so he lets them even keep their guns. The first thing he does is to tell them to choose a new *amghar* as Asardu is almost dead from loss of blood. Then some 1400 sheep are turned over to Si Bu Rahhal, the 790 best of which are to be taken to the *Qa'id* Si Hammu as a sign of the submission of the Ait u-Qantul, while the 600 that remain are to be divided up among the Ait Zaghrar attackers. The newly chosen *amghar* is Bassu, who originally gave the alarm and who is now invested with the *khalifa*'s turban, while lamentations by the women indicate that Asardu has just died. Bassu's pragmatic dictum is that one must see things as they are, *labudd adzghit tigha-siwin lillan r-l-uqt* (ibid.: 118), that God will surely have mercy on Muhammad Asardu, who was indeed a man. But the *khalifa* Si Bu Rahhal is another, with all the virtues of a leader, and now there are no more snakes in the region in any event! (It is difficult to resist adding here the Moroccan Arabic equivalent to the Berber proverb just cited: *had shi lli kayin*, 'That's the way things are!')

In 'Haddou d'Ait Irmog' ('Haddu n-Ait Irmug', 1928), the young man in the title role, Haddu n-Ait Irmug, is an excellent mouflon hunter and is about to marry ʿIzza Hammuda of Ait Arag. But after he returns from a well paid job as a caravan guard in the Dra valley, he learns that ʿIzza has just been married to a certain ʿAli, the nephew of the wealthy *amghar* of Ait Irmug, at Adislan, because the latter offered her father a big sack of duros. So Haddu goes to Ait Arag in a blind rage. Finding himself alone at the *qsar* there, for those who live there are all at ʿAli's parents' house, he sets fire to it while waiting for his would-be father-in-law and his rival to return; but suddenly, in the midst of the flames, a wall falls in on top of him. ʿIzza's father and his son-in-law ʿAli come back and are horrified at the loss of the *qsar*. But they promise to care for the badly wounded Haddu if, when he is cured, he will leave the area for good. But he refuses, and dies, spurning their pity and cursing them for having taken ʿIzza away from him.

In 'La Requisition' ('The Requisition', 1928), a certain ʿAwsa, who is partly black and who was once a bandit and a cattle thief, is now the leader of a *mkhazni* patrol unit sent by Si Hammu l-Glawi, the *qa'id* of Talwat to the Igarnan section of the Imghran, arriving late at night at the house of their *mqaddim* or headman. ʿAwsa grovels in front of the Glawi but acts like a despot when carrying out his orders, always picking up his *sukhra* or bearer's commission when an order is delivered. The local people of the Igarnan have retained a mute hostility to the Glawi, whose exactions have not pleased them. But on this occasion ʿAwsa takes his time about telling the *mqaddim* the reason for his visit, while talk continues about when and if the Glawi will let the Christians come in with their automobiles, electricity and telephones (which in the vernacular are all neologisms: *tumubilat, trisinti wa tilifun*). The discussion now moves on to what the Igarnan have already given the *qa'id*, 20 rams and 100 ewes, as *hadiya*, and ʿAwsa explains that the *qa'id* as well as all the other *qa'id*-s has to furnish further *hadiya* as gifts for the sultan. Someone else adds that the *shaykh* does not give everything to the *qa'id*: when the latter wants a thousand duros, the former demands three times as much, while the *qa'id* either does not know about it or looks the other way. '*Lsin u simm*, tongue and poison', says ʿAwsa, who points out that the Igarnan region is a wealthy one, and also that the village of l-Ahwant, where the action is taking place, is divided into two lineage groups, the smaller one being the Ait Ahnu, of which the *Mqaddim* Kabir is a member, and the larger one being the Ait Sura, who bear three-quarters of the village's expenses. ʿAwsa wants to leave them confused and discontented, and recalls to them that the *Qa'id* Si Hammu had many houses of the people at Targa n-Ada who refused to pay him tribute torn or burned down. He adds that the *qa'id* does not want the French to interfere with this lucrative distraction. So the *Mqaddim* Kabir slips ʿAwsa a fistful of duros before he leaves.

On the *qa'id*'s orders, the *mkhazni* patrol requisitions all the mules in a caravan which is going to the *suq* at Demnat, and their loads are to be given to the *mqaddim* of l-Ahwant to guard, while the muleteers themselves are to go down to Warzazat to work on the French roads. One muleteer, a Berber from Azilal who served in France during World War I, objects to this high-handed treatment and is struck down by a gunbutt, while others, including a few Ait ʿAtta, slip away. ʿAwsa is furious, saying he will take the others all to Talwat and throw them into the Glawi's prison, but then they try – successfully – to bribe him so that he will not tell the *qa'id* what has happened, if each of them gives him some money. Right away he appropriates the new blue jillaba of the group's spokesman; so this man and some others, at least, are let off.

But ʿAwsa and the *mkhazni*-s now return to l-Ahwant to shake down the *mqaddim* properly, which he does to the tune of 300 additional duros, complaining (as many Moroccans evidently did at the time) that paper money is not as good as silver. After this he then tries to take Kabir's mule instead. At this point the enraged *mqaddim* tries to knife him but is held back by his own brother Baha with two *mkhazni*-s. A young girl suddenly appears on the threshold, so ʿAwsa says that instead of the mqaddim's brother Baha leading the mule to Talwat, the girl, Mali, to be his wife, will now do so. The girl is of course terrified when ʿAwsa puts her on the mule and then demands a rug to cover her. The last thing he says to the *mqaddim* before his departure is: 'Not a word about this!' And so the poor *mqaddim* can now, after this very strong-arm 'requisition' (for which 'shakedown' is a better word) and in the face of such Mafia-like tactics, only resign himself to God's will.

The final story, although it is more an essay, 'Doléances' ('Complaints', 1929), is a diatribe by a prisoner of the Glawi both against the latter's exactions and against those French officers who have been duped by him, such as the hakim or *Affaires Indigènes* officer who believes everything his *shawsh* or orderly tells him, for the *shawsh* always favors anyone who has a *shkara ghlida*, a fat purse. By insisting on the retention of this old custom, as Euloge noted, the French administration unconsciously reinforced the discretionary power of traditional Moroccan chiefs. It seems obvious that Euloge himself detested the Glawi as much as did ʿAssu u-Ba Slam, the last great *amghar* of the Ait ʿAtta, who did not surrender to the French until after they broke his and his peoples' heroic resistance to them at the Battle of Bu Gafr in the Saghru in February-March 1933 (cf. Hart 1977, 1984: 164-200), although the reasons for such detestation were not entirely identical in each case. At any rate, it seems certain that because of Euloge's highly critical attitude toward the protectorate administration, its doors were largely closed to him.

The last of Euloge's collections of short stories to be considered here, *Ceux des Hautes Vallées* ('People of the High Valleys', Euloge 1976), contains only two stories which did not appear in either of the foregoing ones. The first of these is the title story, 'Ceux des Hautes Vallées ('People of the High Valleys', 1929). Muhammad Imish and his brother Hsayn of Ait Agamru send out their orphaned nephew ʿAbdu over the high passes down to the *suq* at Bu Maln in order to obtain provisions for what promises to be a very early and hard winter. After six days, then twelve, when he has still not returned, they hear that a couple of men have already died in snowdrifts or by falling into the rushing Asif Mgun river, and they wonder if ʿAbdu will ever return. A seer is asked to divine where he might be, and from her description they deduce that he must be at Ait Imiri. But the old shepherd Ba Tinzar curses her. Then two men of the Ait Bu Gimmaz appear and on the basis of their evidence of having seen him, their identification of him seems positive – although in themselves they are not sure. The disappearance of ʿAbdu also sets Muhammad and Hsayn against each other. Muhammad's younger son Brahim, who wanted to accompany ʿAbdu in the first place but was forbidden to do so because he was needed at home to herd the sheep, goes out, exasperated, to look for ʿAbdu; but he comes back, alone and exhausted, next morning. They finally decide to invite the *tulba'*, the Qur'anic students, in to recite the funeral rites for him.

But before they do so, some more people show up, including an ʿ*attar* or spice merchant who has actually seen ʿAbdu and talked to him. In the midst of this ʿAbdu himself suddenly returns, totally exhausted, to the delirious joy of everyone. He recounts that he was alone and stuck for eleven days in the sheepfold of Isuka, in snowdrifts two meters high; and without the barley he had bought for his mule she would have died. But although he is reeling with fatigue, he does his best not to show it. He has, also, brought back all the provisions he had been asked for – except at the end old Ittu tells him that he forgot the salt! But his reputation as a real man, as an *argaz*, is assured. It might be added that this is almost the only one of René Euloge's stories with a 'happy ending'.

In 'La Fille d'Ighil n'Oro' ('The Girl from Ighil n-Ughu', 1930), the twin sons of old ʿAli w-Idir n-Ait Imdlan, Hanaf and Hisham, are very discontented about their much younger half-brother Salah, who has for the past two years been living with 'the girl from Ighil n-Ughu' (lit., 'the crest of milk'), from further south near Taliwin. Her real name is Tawnza and she has got Salah to do her every bidding. But Salah is his father's favorite son, as his mother died after only a year of marriage. He has already spent most of his inheritance on the girl despite the protestations of his elder twin brothers to the effect that the 'girl from Ighil n-Ughu' is the worst kind of prostitute. They begin to think that the best way to resolve the predicament is for Salah to die, even if he is only twenty, and they are both over forty.

The twin brothers listen to a conversation between Salah and Tawnza in which she taunts him about old Si Muh who offers her things; and then she tries to hit Salah for another 500 duros, this time for her mother; she wants him to obtain his inheritance from his father, and finally inveigles him into giving her his last 700 duros which were supposed to have been used to buy supplies. The twin brothers are convinced that Tawnza has bewitched Salah, and Hanaf thinks that the best way to get rid of him is to have old Dawja, whose daughter he impregnated so that she ended up in a Tarudant whorehouse, give him a bowl of poisoned *asqif* curds at the sheepfold of Ait Tilti. Hisham holds back, however, while Hanaf goes on to add that the best way to get rid of Tawnza is to have the deformed and mentally retarded village dwarf Amushʿal strangle her while she is sleeping on the rooftop, and then throw her body into the cavern of Imi n-Ifis ('the Hyena's Mouth'). There is, in addition, the matter of getting rid of Tawnza's sister Fadila, who looks just like her. However, Hanaf thinks, in fact, that Fadila would do well as his second wife, especially as she does not, in his eyes, at least, have the bad reputation of her sister. In order to give everything a pious appearance they also decide to buy new mats for the mosque and the *talib* (pl. *tulba'*, Qur'anic student and/or schoolmaster, the same as *fqih*) and to sacrifice a ram as a *maʿruf* offering at the shrine of Sidi Nzawt.

But old ʿAli and Salah arrive late at Ait Tilti and Dawja gives the poisoned *asqif* to the former by mistake; and this frightens her so much that she gets terrible diarrhea. Hanaf and Hisham are furious when they hear that their father has died as the result of a complete error and that their young brother Salah is still alive. Meanwhile, Amushʿal now does his job and strangles the girl he thinks is Tawnza, sleeping on the roof, for 500 duros, and then duly throws the body into the Imi n-Ifis cavern. But it turns out that it was the sister Fadila, not Tawnza herself, who was sleeping on the roof, so that she too dies by mistake. The story ends ironically with the plans of the twin brothers miscarrying completely, and Salah and Tawnza still alive.

# COLONIAL AND POSTCOLONIAL MOROCCO

As should be obvious from my synopses of Euloge's work, motivation always stands out very clearly and is very well handled by him, while at the same time, and perhaps for the same reason, his characters seem inexorably driven toward tragedy. In the light of what we have learned from Euloge, I now examine three novels by contemporary, postcolonial Moroccan novelists, all of them Berber-speakers, which deal with the same immediately precolonial and early colonial periods in their own areas: Mohammed Khair-Eddine (d. 1954) for the Sus Valley and the Anti-Atlas, and Moha ou Ali Khettouch and Moha Layid (d. ca. 1994) for the southern slope of the East Central Atlas. One major difference between these younger Moroccan authors on the one hand, and Euloge, Piersuis and Coon on the other, is that the latter were contemporaneous or nearly contemporaneous with the events and the ethnographic background to them that they recorded and described, whereas the two first-mentioned authors are a good two generations removed from them: they are writing about people and events at the time of their grandfathers. The third, on the other hand, is closer to the contemporary scene. I note this purely as an observation, with no intent toward pejorative criticism; but it is an inescapable factor in their writing.

A telling example is provided by the Khair-Eddine novel to be discussed below, for as any anthropologist knows, the memories of informants over three generations tend to become selective with respect to details, i.e., which ones are remembered and which are (conveniently) forgotten, suppressed or obliterated with the passage of time. As will soon become clear, the legendary character of Khair-Eddine's bandit protagonist in *Légende et Vie d'Agoun'Chiche* ('The Legend and Life of Agunshish', Khair-Eddine 1984) is much more marked – as well as consciously stressed – than it is in any of Euloge's or Coon's Berber characters of two generations earlier. It is thus no accident that in Khair-Eddine's excellent novel the factor of 'legend' is given priority over that of 'life', even though it is clear that Agunshish himself, or the individual upon whom he was modeled, was an Anti-Atlas contemporary of the

Imghran and Imgunn *dramatis personae* of the Euloge tales from the Western and Central Atlas watershed. It should also go without saying that in these and other contemporary Moroccan novels the perspective, of course, shifts from that of colonialism to that of anti-colonialism, in addition to the fact that in the latter we are looking quite far backward at the events in question as opposed to looking at them only slightly backward or even directly in the former. The characters themselves may have been almost the same in a *de facto* sense, but the time factor and the shift in emphasis are responsible for an almost radical change in the position of the observer.

Khair-Eddine's novel about Agunshish begins with a long introduction on the impressions of a Susi Berber from the Anti-Atlas (almost certainly himself) returning to his home valley of Tafrawt after a twenty-year absence, an introduction in which he comments, *inter alia*, on the cultural gap between the old men at home who are dying off and the younger ones who have been exposed to urban life in northern Morocco through labor migration. We are then plunged back into the depths of local mythology, as what comes next is an account of the eponymous ancestor of the people of the valley, a nomad named Lahsin Ufughin, who fled the supposed point of origin of the Susis or Ishilhayen at Tamdult n-w-Aqqa after a terrible but unspecified cataclysm hit the region, and then came to Azru w-Adu ('Windy Rock') overlooking the Tafrawt basin. Azru w-Adu was at the time inhabited by only one family, so Lahsin Ufughin married into it, exchanged a large number of sheep and goats for plots of land, and became a sedentary farmer. His descendants swarmed into the Tafrawt and Ammeln valleys, introducing the feud and the vendetta (cf. Hart 1980, 1994) into what was once a peaceful region, in which violent intra-village hatreds now began to develop. Women were never shot at, but as insecurity was permanent, supplies became more and more scarce. The break among Lahsin Ufughin's descendants was caused by a beautiful woman, in whose house two of them were found one night; and they refused to leave. The men outside threatened to burn the house down, as adultery was not then punished by death, adulteresses were not then stoned and their lovers were not then killed. They merely paid a heavy fine and the matter was forgotten. In this particular case, however, the woman happened to be a member of a lineage group which would not accept dishonor, which is why both men were killed and emasculated. The hatred boiling in the hearts of the descendants of Lahsin Ufughin dates from this time although some old men attribute its cause to a north Saharan famine. This was a time, too, when 'bandits of honor' (bandits, social or otherwise) appeared on the scene, with nothing but their mules, rifles, cartridge belts and daggers; and their revolts had ricocheting effects both on themselves and on their families.

As of perhaps about 1910 (although Khair-Eddine is careful not to give dates), one such bandit was named Lahsin Agunshish ('dead tree trunk'), a nickname which he had received after having been pursued by trackers who could not find him and who gave up after finding only an *agunshish*, a dead tree trunk, in a cave. He operated alone but began to take greater risks in raiding *suq*-s and *musim*-s, annual pilgrimages made to saints' shrines; and he also exploited his considerable knowledge of sorcery on simple people and on women. It was said that he became a *tagmart n-isimdal* (lit., 'mare of the cemetery') or unicorn, spreading terror by night wherever he went. (Khair-Eddine notes that the antithesis of the tagmart n-isimdal, which has been recorded in all Berber cultures, is al-Buraq, the human-headed horse held by Muslims to have transported the Prophet miraculously from Medina to Jerusalem in a single night. 'Al-Buraq symbolized the force and power of God the creator, while tagmart n-isimdal was related to the maleficent forces of darkness': ibid.: 30.) Agunshish was afraid of nobody, and although months or even years might go by in which he did not kill anyone, whenever he decided to finish with an enemy he did so promptly. He only used firearms to impress a crowd and would single out one of his trackers in a large crowd of people and then shoot him unerringly in the head. The confusion which resulted gave him the opportunity to slip away like ectoplasm. At other times he would doctor his enemies' tea, but only those who really knew would realize that the responsibility for their deaths was his. He would approach a tea merchant and tell him to put a few drops of viper venom in the tea of Flan u-Flan, for, if he did not, Agunshish would then return and kill him.

Harking for a moment back to Euloge's story about Bassu n-Ait u-Qantul, there was even a whole lineage group in the region whose members specialized in the extraction of poison from horned vipers, and one member of one of its three main branches, nicknamed 'the Violator' ('*le Violeur*'), also specialized in raping single women so as to appropriate their property without the burden of having to marry them – although *a priori* it is difficult if not impossible to see just how he might have accomplished such a feat, particularly in defiance of both Shari$^c$a and customary law regulations on the matter! He was also an excellent shot, eliminating most of the members of an opposing lineage and then, with his brothers, finally succeeding in banishing it from his village. At this point there follow a number of anecdotes about the baraka of Sidi Ahmad u-Musa, one of the most important saints of the Anti-Atlas, along with a nice analysis of why magic, sorcery and witchcraft cannot possibly be considered pre-Islamic, as they are manifestations of divine will (ibid.: 39). Khair-Eddine also shows why bandits like Agunshish could fit into the life of a community, but why they did not do so very well.

In conclave with his two brothers, the Violator decides that he wants to go north to buy a repeating rifle, as Agunshish has a good English one, offered to him by a cousin in Tangier who had to flee there in exile from a feud at home. They discuss Agunshish, and characterize him as a calm, tranquil and good man who would never have killed anyone if his sister had not been killed. He has sworn to kill all the men of the village of her murderer, and has already accounted for over a dozen. He is very punctilious and will either kill all his enemies or be killed himself, although he has never killed nor robbed innocent travelers. He eats his quota of meat through hunting mouflon, and is in no sense a 'hired killer'.

At this point the Violator and his brothers hear a number of shots fired several hundred meters away and with binoculars they see that some six armed men have surrounded Agunshish in the mountains. One of these men has already been hit in the leg, so the Violator and his brothers decide to help Agunshish by firing long shots from their own positions. They down two more men in this fashion. Three remain, and Agunshish kills one of them. The last two, not knowing what has hit them, run away.

The Violator now wants Agunshish to accompany him to the Gharb (i.e., the northern cities and coastal plains of Atlantic Morocco), so they stop at the tomb of Sidi ʿAbd al-Jabbar before leaving the Ammeln valley, and sacrifice two bulls there. They spend the night inside the sanctuary of the shrine, and hand out the meat in one-kilogram lots to those who come to offer prayers for them on their perilous venture to come. So they pick up their mules and rifles from an old gunsmith and head north. While hunting rabbits at night in the countryside, the Violator refrains from killing a crazy woman who has been chased out of her village. After a might's sleep, he and Agunshish discuss their dreams. Further along the Violator sees an attractive young girl and goes after her, and then hears a shot when Agunshish roars at him to stay away from his daughter!

This trip taken by Agunshish and the Violator north to the Gharb probably occurred about 1916-1917, when a local strongman named Hayda u-Mwis (possibly 'Hayda Son of his Mother', implying illegitimacy because of an unknown father?), the pasha of Tasrudant, was operating, under French colonial manipulation, in the Sus valley, until he was killed by the Ait Ba ʿAmran, who suspended his head from an *argan* tree which was thenceforth known as *Targant n-Hayda u-Mwis*, 'the small argan tree of Hayda u-Mwis'. At any rate,

Agunshish's daughter wants her father to come home, at which point her mother also appears. Agunshish assures them that he will indeed come home once he has done what he has to do in the Gharb.

There is also a considerable amount of dreaming and dream analysis and interpretation of the parts both of Agunshish and the Violator, each usually telling the other that his interpretations are wrong (for dreams and dream interpretations in Morocco, cf. Kilborne 1978)! As the blurb on the back cover of Khair-Eddine's novel says, 'we are confronted with a very blurred historical period, one very propitious for legends and the supernatural' – and not for nothing, as noted, does the word *legende* precede that of *vie* in the title – 'but it is in contact with the colonial invader the closer our heroes come to descending into the plain'. One might even venture to say that there is much in this picaresque novel that is reminiscent of Cervantes' *Don Quijote*.

A young female demon, a *tajinnit*, now invites Agunshish and the Violator into a sumptuous cavern. She tells Agunshish that he will never see his dead sister again and that if he does he will go crazy. The memory of what happened comes back to him, that he avenged her death by killing her murderer; but her memory will not go away. Then they leave the cavern and come upon the valley of the Wad Sus near Tarudant, which was at the time both the economic and spiritual capital of the Sus region (although this is no longer the case today). French colonization had already begun by this time, although the Anti-Atlas and the Ait Ba ʿAmran were still in dissidence and would remain so until 1934. The French administration, as noted, sent out an expedition against the Ait Ba ʿAmran headed by Hayda u-Mwis, but unfortunately even the latter's head resting in an argan tree did not disturb the colonizers' plans and only served to multiply the French alliance with other *qa'id*-s. Some months later, indeed, they bombarded the villages and *suq*-s of the Anti-Atlas from the air, exactly as they had done in the Rif before bin ʿAbd al-Krim surrendered.

At Tarudant Agunshish and the Violator are halted by a lieutenant of the legion, but as they have already hidden their arms, they are allowed to pass through when they say that they are grain merchants doing business in the market and at Ait Baha. While in their hostelry they save the life of an escaped prisoner and former *qa'id* at Igharm, in the country of the Id aw-Kansus tribe, who was replaced by a lieutenant of Hayda u-Mwis. This man was then poisoned by a woman on the *qa'id*'s orders, and he himself had also just been wounded in an ambush. They figure that the best way he can escape from Tarudant is to be disguised as a woman, and they buy the necessary clothes from a merchant who has just returned from the north. And so they all leave

Tarudant, but a band of slavers led by a black named, appropriately, Bismgan (Tsh. *ismag*, pl. *isimgan*, 'black') is soon on their heels. They kill his men, and wound and capture him, promising him his life only if he will turn over to them the ransom money he gained through previous extortions and sale of slaves.

In this way they arrive at the *qa'id*'s village in the mountains near Igharm, where they are well received and where even the old men have heard of Agunshish's exploits. His praises are sung and Bismgan's savage slavery activities are reviled by the *ra'is* or leader of the *ahwash* song and dance group in the courtyard, after a good dinner washed down with mint tea. After breakfast next morning the *qa'id*'s stronghold suffers some French air bombardment, but only a donkey is killed, while the *qa'id*, Agunshish and the Violator shoot at the planes with rifles. But the bombing is a sign that the French want unconditional surrender. Indeed some villages have already surrendered and are hence considered as traitors and cowards by those which have not, even though it is known that they would have had no chance against well-armed goums from among their own people in French service.

The colonizers have occupied conquered territory and appointed *qa'id*-s favorable to them and supervised by their military; but they are also respecting the customary law of each tribe and have brought provisions and medication. all of which has greatly facilitated their penetration. More and more people are beginning to think that it would be better to treat with them than to live in perpetual dissidence, but the big *qa'id*-s of the confines have not agreed enough among themselves to arrive at a lasting accord. At this point a runner arrives saying that a meeting is to be held in the Ait ʿAbdallah. In the face of a modern European invasion these Berbers do not want to lose their identity, their culture or anything else of importance to them.

The next day on their way to Ait ʿAbdallah they find that the *suq* of Jumaʿ Aqdim has been bombed from the air and that a massacre has resulted. Ait Baha has already been occupied and a piste is under construction to Tafrawt. Many tribes have already been betrayed by their own imgharen, who were given arms by the French and then sold them at several times their value to the dissidents in the mountains. The *qa'id* whom Agunshish has befriended offers him either his mare – but Agunshish values his she-mule too much to accept her – or a girl to marry; but he accepts only the *qa'id*'s friendship. And in yet another vision he sees that he will fight to the death, as there is nothing left for him to do in this world.

It turns out that the tribal meeting of the aitarbiʿin at Ait ʿAbdallah was very stormy, with several defections by *qa'id*-s who thought that they could deal more profitably with the colonizers on their own and hence forced their people to surrender. Then the French army encircled the Ait ʿAbdallah and beat them in battle, signed the peace with the local *qa'id*, who retained his job, and marched on to Tafrawt where there was no fighting at all and where nobody kept their arms except the imgharen, the *qa'id*-s and a few bandits like Agunshish who would never surrender in any case. The Violator has now become *amghar* of the Ammeln, but only for a short time and because he is allowed to carry a shotgun.

It is now 1934, and Agunshish is alone. There is as yet no price on his head but he can no longer appear in the *suq*-s and he must hide in order to avoid capture and death. He is also running very low on ammunition, and can only go to the markets disguised as a Sahrawi or a beggar. Although with peace a new prosperity has come, and returned emigres from the north are building bigger houses, Agunshish has only been able to visit his family at night, now that his nephews have become businessmen in a northern city. It is ever harder for him to live on his own off the land, as game has become very scarce, so he finally goes to Tiznit, despite the presence there of French cars and machinery, all of which he detests. He also watches the execution of a mentally retarded giant falsely accused of having raped and shot the wife of a French captain. Gritting his teeth, he resolves to enter the world of the colonizer, a world where only money counts, as he is obliged to live in it. If he cannot lick them, he will join them; but he will do so only on his own terms, for the secret, he holds, is to observe without ever letting anyone know what one is thinking. (There are still a few resistants left like the *Qa'id* Najim al-Akhsasi, who was promised arms by the Spanish when they occupied Ifni in 1934, but even when he went to Madrid to see Franco, they failed to deliver!) And so, when a truck runs over his mule in his absence, he comes back to find her suffering horribly; and he therefore has to kill her with his knife. He does so with tears running down his cheeks, and then he buries her with his own hands so that her body will not be eaten by dogs or vultures. He decides then and there never again to return to the mountains of his birth, and he buries his weapons beside his mule. Then he takes the bus to Casablanca.

In this splendid book Khair-Eddine has truly written a winner, a superb piece of literary ethnography in which the natural and the visible are beautifully merged with the supernatural and the invisible, and the overall context of Islam, as manifested at least in southwestern Morocco, is ever-present. The time perspective, one begins to feel, becomes quite necessary in order to add substance to the legend.

The more recent novel of Moha ou Ali Khettouch, *Azour Amokrane Ne Meurt Jamais...* ('Azur Amqqran Will Never Die...,' Khettouch 1991) is much shorter than the Khair-Eddine work, and about the same length as one of Euloge's longer short stories; and indeed it might have been cut still further as it contains a good deal of extraneous and non-essential material even so. But what is not extraneous is very worthwhile, for the book is a disguised and informal history of the tribe of the Ait Murghad on the southern slope of the East-Central Atlas, from the time of Mawlay al-Hasan I (1873-94) until well into the French protectorate period. (For a historical survey of the region at large during this time, cf. Dunn 1977). During the reign of Mawlay al-Hasan I, it seems that a certain ʿAli w-ʿAssu of the Ait Hammi lineage of the Ait ʿAmr u-Mansur section of the Ait Murghad, domiciled at Awrir, received confirmation by sultanic decree or *zahir* of his *de facto qa'id*-ship of the Ait Murghad and the Qabbala (oasis-dwelling blacks, synonymous with *haratin*) of Tadighust and Amsid; and the Ait Murghad prospered under his tutelage. But he had an enemy living further south, a 'brigand' (the author's term: probably more likely a local strongman) named Baba n-Ait ʿAli, a petty tyrant who ordered people to be executed right and left, a man of lightning changes of mood who was capable of committing horrible atrocities for no apparent reason. He adored women, and when one of his favorites had her toe stepped on by a goat, he had the whole herd of 300 goats slaughtered in front of their owner. But then the good *amghar* ʿAli w-ʿAssu died, at over 80 years of age, and Baba n-Ait ʿAli was murdered by his own mercenaries at Tulwin n-ʿArab s-Sibbah.

Hsayn w-ʿAli n-Ait ʿAssu succeeded his father as *qa'id*, and was generally also regarded as a good man. But he had no sons and only one daughter, Tuda, and died aged only fifty without making a will. Tuda Hsayn was married first to her patri-parallel cousin, but they were soon divorced because of mutual dislike. Then she married another young man named ʿAddi, also of the Ait Hammi lineage, in a big wedding with singing, *ahidus* dancing and recitations by the *imdyazen*, professional (as well as endogamous and low-class) musicians, all of which is given due ethnographic description. She then had a miscarriage, but ten months later gave birth to a boy.

However, the French invasion now began from the southeast and the Algerian frontier, starting at Bu Dnib, in 1912, and all the Ait Murghad sections concluded a pact of alliance against them. This pact Khettouch refers to as *tada*, which he describes as a pact of co-lactation (ibid.: 40), exactly as Marcy described it for the Aith Ndhir of the Middle Atlas (Marcy 1936), a pact which, incidentally, among the Ait ʿAtta, the local arch-enemies of the Ait

Murghad, was known as *tafargant* (Hart 1981: 188-89, and 1984: 63-5). And here it may be worth injecting some local notions of sociopolitical relations: Khettouch notes also that if an u-Murghad, an individual of the Ait Murghad, wanted to ally himself by tada with an u-Hadiddu, or individual of the Ait Hadiddu – another neighboring tribal group with membership in the Ait Yafalman confederacy, a membership also claimed by the Ait Murghad –, then each *takat* or nuclear family of the Ait Murghad had to ally itself with a corresponding *takat* of the Ait Hadiddu. The two tribes thus became, integrally, 'brothers' through *tada*, on the basis that what works for individuals works even better for groups; and the tada relationship, thus formalized, was now ratified by the councils of both tribes in front of a saint's shrine. When the French 'pacification' came, this pact was turned automatically into one of jihad, of holy war (Khettouch 1991: 40).

The Battle of Win Iwalyun on August 31, 1930, was hard fought and ended with the French entry into Igulmimen (Gulmima) on September 15 of the same year. The Ait Murghad, including Hsayn w-ᶜAddi n-Ait Hammi, now grown up, and his family, now moved south to Alnif at the eastern end of the Saghru in order to conclude an alliance with the Ait ᶜAtta, their irreconcilable enemies prior to 'pacification'; and Khettouch maintains that they joined the great Ait ᶜAtta resistant ᶜAssu u-Ba Slam there in 1932 and that Hsayn w-ᶜAddi n-Ait Hammi (of the Ait Murghad) became one of his most trusted subordinates (ibid.: 48-50). Here I must record my own disagreement: I feel that Khettouch greatly overplays what was at best a very minor role taken by the Ait Murghad in the Ait ᶜAtta resistance to the French which culminated in the great Battle of Bu Gafr in the Saghru in February-March 1933, if indeed they played any such role at all. Furthermore, Khettouch's claim that the Bu Gafr battle completely cleared up all remaining hostility between the Ait ᶜAtta and the Ait Murghad was not corroborated by my own Ait ᶜAtta informants.

With the Ait Murghad, who are obviously his own people, Khettouch is on considerably firmer ground, and he now introduces the famous Ait Murghad bandit Zayd u-Hmad, of the Irbiben (lit:, 'adopted children') section, in 1934 (cf. also Hart 1987: 31-6) after Hsayn w-ᶜAddi and his family reputedly returned home from Bu Gafr, as well as the valiant final resistance of the Ait Murghad themselves at Baddu in the East-Central Atlas in August-September 1933. Zayd u-Hmad was working in corvee labor on the road, and had an altercation with his French foreman in which the latter slapped him. He immediately vowed vengeance, and left to find his old Chassepot rifle with which, it seems, he had already shot down two French aviators in 1932 (a claim which appears exaggerated). The following day he was absent from work but made up for it by shooting both his ex-foreman and a French AI officer in charge of a *harka* which was out to capture him. He even came into the French post at Tinghir and shot a Jew who ran a bar there for the French military, as well as five foreign legionnaires who were drinking there. But he was finally killed at Tadafalt n-Ait ʿAtta in March 1936, where he had friends, after another AI officer confused Tadafalt n-Ignawen (the *qsar* in question) with Taghya n-Ilimshan, both of which are Ait ʿAtta settlements, the latter having been, indeed, the birthplace of ʿAssu u-Ba Slam.

Hsayn w-ʿAddi was a passive spectator at these events, but he resolved that the epoch and epic of Zayd u-Hmad would not remain without a future. He became more religious, and the saint Ba Sidi begged him to give more time for payment to all his debtors. In a generous gesture, he absolved them all completely, and the absolution was followed not only by a full recitation of the Qur'an but by that of the litany of the Darqawa religious order. After this, in a good and abundant year, Hsayn w-ʿAddi put his house and property in order. But then he began to have dissensions with his second wife, Ittu, so he divorced her, and then took a third wife from outside his own lineage group. Ittu gave birth six months later to a son, Itri (lit., 'star'), who was brought to Awrir and educated in a fine Qur'anic school under *Talib* Muh, where he did very well, especially under pressure, as *Talib* Muh himself was wont to inflict heavy punishment with his cane on inept or recalcitrant pupils. Nonetheless, he was generally regarded as very just. One extremely poor student, Ha w-ʿAli u-Baha, put a scorpion inside his slipper when made to repeat a hundred times what he had failed to learn; but after the scorpion stung *Talib* Muh, he killed it, sucked out the poison and went directly to pray in the mosque. The astonished pupil confessed and was asked to name his own punishment, whipping, which was duly and not unjustly administered by the *talib* himself. He also cured a girl of the *jinn* lurking inside her.

But Itri, living up to his name, indeed proved a star pupil in the school run by *Talib* Muh, and by the age of eight he had learned the whole of the Qur'an. After this he became the youngest tribal scholar and indeed a kind of tribal oracle, to whom all the conflicts in the local community were submitted for judgment. This fact came to the attention of the local French administration, with the AI major in control of the Gulmima and Tadighust district backing him. But the latter's superior officer at Qsar s-Suq opposed his selection as *qa'id* of the Ait Murghad of the Asif n-Ghris. The decision was submitted to a vote, Itri against the other contender, Hammu; and Itri gained a resounding 95 per cent majority. So young Itri became the top chief or *amghar n-ufilla* of the Ait Murghad of the Ghris, supervising the elections of his local *imgharen* n-tmazirt or section chiefs, and of his *imgharen n-w-aman* or irrigation chiefs; and thus he became the 'living incarnation' of the old tribal patriarch ʿAli w-ʿAssu. The final chapter of this novelette ends with the same phrase as all the others '... The almond trees of the Sighnis will never die, and neither will *azur amqqran*'. It should be noted that *azur amqqran*, the title phrase, means 'good root' in Tamazight Berber, and the appellation refers, of course, to the continuity of the Ait Hammi lineage of the Ait Murghad. The plot line needs considerably more fleshing out, but the work does have historical and ethnographic value. Perhaps a sequel to it may take us on to Moroccan independence in 1956, and into the postcolonial era.

An even more recent novel by another author who is also from the Ait Murghad, Moha Layid, *Le Sacrifice des Vaches Noires* ('The Sacrifice of the Black Cows', Layid 1993), however, brings the fortunes of at least a part of that tribe up to the time of Moroccan independence. Although the story line in Layid's novel is also rather thin, this fact is more than adequately compensated for by the texture, at once rich and sensitive, of his ethnography, threads of which are to be found on almost every page of his text, one which in my view represents a considerable ethnographic achievement. Indeed, it is not too much to say that in this case the ethnography carries the story.

The action begins in the Tinjdad oasis in the late summer of 1953, after the enforced exile, by the French colonialists, of the Moroccan sultan Sidi Muhammad bin Yusuf to Madagascar. The oasis is suffering from a major drought which an old widower named Bassu is trying to think of some way to overcome. He recalls many previous droughts in his near-century of existence, but none as bad as this one. A factor which seems to have hastened it, if not entirely brought it on, is the recent introduction of motorized water pumps, brought down from the north by migrant workers from the region, who in putting them to work have, he considers, dried up its springs and wells. In earlier days, he recalls, everything could be taken care of by praying in the mosque and then by sacrificing one or two black cows in the riverbed, a solution which almost always worked for people who were patient and of good faith. But nowadays, he ruminates, while sitting under a tamarisk that is even older than he is, nobody is interested – or disinterested – and therefore the goodness and the bounty of God are perhaps becoming scarcer commodities.

Bassu then goes to his married daughter ʿAisha, her husband Lahsin (who is only sixty) and his three grandchildren for dinner. Here he learns that the parents of Yidir, even though suffering particularly badly from the drought, have nonetheless recently celebrated the marriage of their son (while in

Bassu's view they are paying for the sins of their ancestors). Old Bassu has an idea on his way home and goes to the mosque to tell Si Lahsin the *fqih* about it. On the way out, he meets Yidir himself, who is also the nephew of a resistant at the 1933 Battle of Baddu against the French. Yidir is now married, but of fairly frail physique, and if he should die, all the brothers of his father Muha w-ᶜAli n-Ait Yidir would only await the latter's death so as to be able to claim their share of the inheritance.

Although Yidir is tired of the oasis, Bassu persuades him not to go to any of the northern cities to look for work. He tells him of his misgivings about the water pumps and promises to give him 1000 francs for every pump he manages to destroy. At this point even Yidir's young wife Ittu knows that without his father's patrimony her husband would be nothing, and she has a hard time supporting her mother-in-law Hadda. Yidir, however, is convinced by old Bassu's arguments and tells his wife that he must renounce his plans to go north and must look instead for work on the road gang under the French. At least this way he will remain close to her physically, and he remembers that on one occasion when the pumps were closed down, the Tudgha River flowed much more freely. He realizes that the owners of the pumps have received subventions because they cultivated a few date palms while killing off thousands of others which were several hundred years old; and he makes this observation to Bassu, who sees that a bond has now been formed between Yidir and himself.

So Yidir goes out at night to set the first of the diesel pumps on fire – successfully, too, as there is an explosion and the flames rise high – after which he returns home quietly. The result next morning is the surprise and stupor of all the *qsar* dwellers at the burning of the pump: they are sure it must have been done by some jealous property owner whose well was always dry or whose pump was out of order. In any case, Hammu, the man whose pump was destroyed, is held by the rest of the villagers to be a pretentious ignoramus who has received his just desserts and who is once again at the near-starvation level of the rest of the *qsar*. Yidir, however, now remains quiet for the next two weeks while working on the road. But he decides to avoid meeting any victims of future pump fires, and he remembers Bassu's words: 'All these people need water and although we cannot fight the sirocco we can help to stop the harmful work of men'. With this in mind, Yidir now goes out again at night to burn another pump, for which Bassu secretly gives him 2000 francs.

The French Affaires Indigènes captain at the Tinjdad post now wants to organize a local militia to act as an anti-incendiary squad. He hopes that by so doing this might help to keep the minds of some of the young men away from nationalistic thoughts, for which several of their number have already been jailed and put to forced labor. He and his paramilitary *mkhazni*-s tell the local *shaykh*-s that they are responsible for what is happening in the oasis, and that he does not want them to listen to any workers who have come back from the north with seditious ideas, for it is now two months since the first fires began. The AI captain has his brigadier (*l-birgadi*) of *mkhazni*-s, an Indo-Chinese war veteran named Hmad, ready to carry out his orders, for he thinks the fires are an integral part of 'nationalist terrorism'. Meanwhile, Yidir is more and more often away from home, working on the road by day and secretly burning the pumps at night. His father Muha w-ʿAli is sure that the 400 frs. that his son earns per day on the road is far from covering all his expenses, while his wife Ittu also is beginning to wonder what is going on and why her husband seems to be so tired so often. (As noted earlier, for a discussion of a similar situation in Algeria, one in which forest fires served as a device to combat French colonialism, cf. Prochaska 1986.)

The AI captain may not like the fact of illiterate tribesmen defying his authority, but he is also beginning to have major doubts about the purpose of his mission in Morocco. He was himself in the French resistance against the Germans during World War II, then in Indo-China, and he now begins to wonder if the Moroccan nationalists are not fighting French authority in the same way that the French fought against the Germans. So, in private at least, he makes no bones about his respect and admiration for the nationalists. In this captain, we have a silhouette, if not a portrait, by a Moroccan author of a French colonialist soldier who is by no means 'all bad': he has a job to do, even though he may not like it and/or may have become personally estranged from it.

Ittu has now been pregnant for six months, and her husband's parents are delighted. She is made to take all sorts of local medicines and herbs to hasten the birth of a boy (such as eating a hedgehog so that her son will be as crafty as Berber legend holds that animal to be). She agrees to take two candles to the shrine of Sidi Bu l-Man (Bulman) and embrace his tomb seven times so that she will have a son.

Yidir goes out again at night and suddenly runs into a small group of men who are nationalists and who know what he is up to.. They say that they will not denounce him to the captain if he accepts their conditions, the first of which is to say nothing about the fact that he has seen them either to the *shaykh* or to his wife – and then two more pumps are burned. Yidir starts to have nightmares and now himself secretly burns a candle at the tomb of Sidi Bu l-Man.

Yidir's father Muha w-ᶜAli is ailing and slowly dying, while his wife's pregnancy increases and while the people are putting money aside to buy black cows to sacrifice so that the thin thread of water in the river will grow stronger. Herewith I make a direct quote in translation (Layid 1993: 99): 'Yidir in any case was unable to rid himself of certain beliefs anchored in his spirit like the indelible traces of a tattoo... It was stronger than he was, even if he had proven that the blood of the cows sacrificed was the consequence and not the cause of the appearance of a thin trickle of water... True causes are often ignored by men who prefer those, often false, which assure the cohesion of the social group. Yidir knew that his actions were more efficacious than all the incantations or other sacrifices. It was the fires that he had lit which forced the water to run as it did at present in the river bed. "We separate the dead from the living and the living from the dead" (Qur'an, Sura of the Cow, Verse 77)'.

The ethnographic implications with respect to ritual and belief in this quotation may be compared and contrasted to another, further on (ibid.: 109): 'The sacrifice of the black cows had certainly served some purpose, or so the *qsar* dwellers thought. These were infallible ancestral recipes, and when the results were negative, it was because the participants had not respected all the rules of the ritual.' This same issue, in one form or another, becomes one of the major features of Layid's ethnography, playing, as it does, on and around the theme of the distinction made by Gellner between Islam of the Book and Islam of the Shrine (Gellner 1969: 5-12, Gellner 1984), despite the fact that it is not couched in these terms.

To continue, however, a curfew is now imposed on the *qsar*. But that same night Yidir meets three nationalists, all unknown to him, and tells them he is with them and their cause, the orders for which come ultimately from Rabat and the absent sultan Sidi Muhammad bin Yusuf. The resistants tell him to keep on burning the pumps for the good of the cause, as a number of their comrades have already been jailed and sent to forced labor at Aghbalu n-Kardus, some 60 km. to the northwest, into the Central Atlas.

Yidir's father is now too sick to leave his home, and the charm in writing that the *fqih* has given him has had little effect. Visitors also urge Yidir and his pregnant wife to look after his mother, while Ittu secretly hopes her father-in-law will die, so that if his mother then continues to live with them she will have to conform more to their ways. Yidir meanwhile goes out less and less to work on the road. His father tells him not to pay any more money to cure him, only to put aside enough for his funeral, and to show fortitude in front of the women and to sacrifice a sheep the day he dies. He wants the *fqih* to come and draw up a list of his creditors, whom he has instructed Yidir to pay. There is no doubt that Yidir has grown up a great deal in the year since his marriage, for which his father had to sell their cow, in order to meet the wedding expenses; but old Bassu tells him to come to him again if he needs money.

Yidir's son Muha is finally born, to the sound of rejoicing and female ululation, so his father is now ready to die in peace. The women, who dominate the proceedings, bring Ittu a bowl of date bouillon: the room is full of them, for, as Layid notes, birth is a women's affair while death is the province of men, with life itself existing between the two (ibid.: 131, 135). The sheep is slaughtered next morning, and when the men are congratulating Yidir, Bassu slips him a small purse containing 30,000 francs. That same evening Yidir's father dies after having been a grandfather for several hours. The *tulba'* (Qur'anic students) and the *fqih* come to recite the Qur'an and to wash and enshroud the body, which is then taken to the cemetery next morning. Ittu cannot conceal her delight over the birth of her son, but is able to conceal it over the death of her father-in-law. She cannot take part in the mourning, however, because the *jnun* (pl. of *jinn*) do not approve if a woman who has just given birth starts to lament. Three days of mourning are observed, and then it is over.

Some days later Yidir is visited by two men whom he does not know and who want to have a whole sack of sugar sent over to him: they are nationalists and when the doors are closed, they ask him to join them and continue the struggle, and not to let up until the French let Sidi Muhammad bin Yusuf return from 'Madame Gascar'. They tell him he is to be a courier, a dispatch-runner – at which point the sack of sugar is brought in and mint tea is served. For three months now Yidir assumes a liaison with a *qsar* halfway between Tinjdad and Aghbalu n-Kardus in order to get directives from the local resistance leaders, of whom, he has only seen three so far, with their turbans covering their faces; but he marches all night with messages to the next courier, for he knows he is doing the right thing in working for his country's independence. He wonders that if he is arrested Ittu will be able to resist misery and deprivation. She is already herself wondering about his nocturnal absences, and early one morning he comes back home to sleep, wakes up and finds out from his mother that Ittu has returned to her parents' house. So he goes to his parents-in-law with the *shaykh* of the *qsar* and Si Lahsin the *fqih*, and after the latter has made some appropriate recitations from the Qur'an, Yidir takes Ittu home and explains his nocturnal absences by telling her that he is a contraband dealer in *kif*, asking her to ask him no more questions – even though he feels ashamed at having had to lie to her.

By this time, too, only a few pumps are left in the oasis, and those who own them are trying to sell them at low prices, given the fire hazard – while old Bassu has at last discovered that the sacrifice of black cows in the riverbed has had no effect on the drought. The curfew is still maintained and everybody hurries home so as not to be outside the *qsar* once it begins at dusk. Bassu asks his grandchildren and Yidir to be ready to do some plowing for him next day. But Yidir, who is taking messages to prisoners at Aghbalu n-Kardus, is intercepted on the path by a *mkhazni* patrol under Brigadier Hmad of the AI 'bureau', for which act the brigadier receives two sacks of sugar and a promotion to *shawsh*. Something breaks inside old Bassu on hearing this news, and he falls down in his field while showing his grandchildren how to sow grain. He is taken home, dies there and is buried near Muha w-ᶜAli n-Ait Yidir.

Ittu weeps over her husband's incarceration, while his mother Hadda is physically unable to take on all the housework – but a day later she starts to accompany Ittu to the prison to take Yidir his meals. Nonetheless, the presence of the brigadier at mealtimes bothers Yidir so much that he forbids his wife to come to him, telling her that she is better off staying at home, where the whole *qsar* can watch over her.

The captain himself is not in top form either and he remembers his own experiences with the SS guards in a Nazi jail: he is like a devil in the mornings and a near-angel in the afternoons. Through the schoolmistress, his wife distributes clothing and a little money to the children of the political prisoners. He tells her that if this intolerable situation continues, he, who only drinks sparingly, might well become an alcoholic. The actions of the Moroccan resistants remind him irresistibly of his own actions during the war, and for this reason he has never been able to maltreat prisoners physically.

The captain decides to turn Yidir into his gardener, as he speaks some French and has been to primary school. Yidir agrees to do so if he can see his wife once a week and receive his meals from his mother. The captain's wife sends him bread and jam as well. The other prisoners start being sarcastic to him as a result, and he is rejected by all of them, including those of the resistance. But he asks his mother to light some candles at the shrine of Sidi Bu l-Man and to promise the saint the sacrifice of a black cow after he obtains his freedom. He does so, but cautiously, so that possible enemies may not spot her actions. At the cemetery, too, she reproaches her dead husband at his grave for having left them only misery, debts and bad memories. She regrets that her grandson bears his name and hopes that the hyenas will devour his bones.

Every Monday Ittu now goes to the captain's garden to take Yidir his lunch, but during the initial visits the sentry does not let her approach him. However, one day the captain's wife sees them and asks her husband to let Ittu see Yidir and to let them eat their lunch together under a big apricot tree.

So the very first time they are together, after a year of deprivation, they have frenzied sex — a state of affairs which now continues once a week. Two months later Ittu tells Yidir she is pregnant again, and three months later she begins to show it. All the villagers know about her pregnancy and are sure she will have a bastard child, possibly even a Christian *jinn*, as some of them think she has become the captain's mistress. But after the explanations given by Yidir, his mother Hadda knows that the child will be his, despite vicious village gossip (one man in particular saying he has heard that Christian *jnun* are especially fond of the blood of black cows).

Only four people have admitted the correlation between the destruction of the pumps and the abundance of water: the late Bassu, Yidir, Ittu and the captain. The first two can no longer say anything and the officer thinks the *qsar* would revolt if the truth were revealed. As for Ittu, she has become delirious and nobody can take her seriously. During lucid moments she says she was wrong to go against the current and oppose everyone: if the *qsar* dwellers hold the blood of black cows to be capable of stooping a drought, why should she argue to the contrary? A truth defended by a minority is a lie until a majority believes and adheres to it: the truth is what people believe, not what is (ibid.: 187).

The captain's wife, reliving her own first years of love, and not just as a voyeuse, takes pictures from her kitchen window of Yidir and Ittu in the middle of the sex act, but she does not know of the drama that Ittu is currently undergoing, as a result of the village belief that the *jnun* have taken over her body because of her supposed fornication and that God is now punishing her as a result. The Frenchwoman, on hearing this, knows that it is patently false: she has the proof, and she wants to give Yidir the photographs that she has taken. He looks at them later, is delighted with them as they will stop any further malicious gossip, and puts the best one in an envelope for his mother to give to the *fqih*, with a letter saying that he has found far more sympathy and understanding from the wife of a French officer than from his own fellow tribesmen, and to tell them that a foreign lady has given him not necessarily the means of curing his wife but of saving her honor. Even the *fqih* begins to weep over this, and tells Hadda that he will make the news public right away.

Hadda now has a dream of good augury for Yidir and Ittu, and tells her son about it. He feels great joy at this and promises in future never to qualify as irrational the behavior of men who are struggling desperately to survive. He passes a letter saying that he is a political detainee working for Moroccan freedom on to a group of French tourists but the sentry grabs him and throws him into a special cell for troublemakers. When he is let out of solitary confinement after ten days of undernourishment, he finds that he is regarded now as a real hero and a patriot by the other prisoners. But at this point he is transferred to the regional prison at Qsar s-Suq, where he finds himself among 40 other political detainees. His new jailer tends to be harsh only when the French are around, but is in reality another resistant, the liaison man between the local resistance and the political prisoners. Yidir is then sent to work in the lime pits, a very much rougher task than being the captain's gardener.

He now receives a letter from his mother saying she has bought a black calf which she will have sacrificed at Sidi Bu l-Man at the right time so that Ittu can regain her reason. The *fqih* has already announced that Ittu's child is indeed her son's, Yidir's, and she is now getting much hidden assistance from the villagers. Then Yidir hears that Ittu has borne him a daughter, appropriately named Hurriya ('freedom') – and gradually the treatment of the prisoners starts to ease up. Then one Friday it is announced that the return of Sidi Muhammad bin Yusuf is imminent. Everyone is overjoyed, and prayers are said for the sultan in the mosque.

But in fact several more months go by before the sultan's return in mid-November 1955. When this happens the prisoners are put into a truck and taken back to Tinjdad where Yidir hopes to see and settle accounts with his enemy Brigadier Hmad who was responsible for jailing him originally; but the brigadier is unfortunately not present. Nonetheless, the crowd is delirious with joy at the arrival of the prisoners, and Ittu gradually yields to Yidir's embraces after he gets home. At home too he learns that not only is the *fqih* Si Lahsin a nationalist but, to his great surprise, that Brigadier Hmad is one as well, as he had the *fqih*'s letters delivered to Yidir when the latter was at Qsar s-Suq. Brigadier Hmad had to make an example of Yidir so as not to fall under French suspicion himself: he was also the third resistant, unrecognized at the time by Yidir, whom the latter met originally at night when he first consented to become a courier. And he has now gone to Rabat to greet Sidi Muhammad bin Yusuf (later to become King Muhammad v) after his long absence. The French captain has been transferred to Algeria, and his wife and children have gone back to France – but Yidir thinks of her with great fondness.

Yidir tells his mother he is going to pray for Ittu's complete return to reason, which according to his mother she lost because she blasphemed by telling all and sundry that the sacrifice of black cows had nothing to do with the problem of water in the oasis, that it was her husband who struggled successfully against the drought and that the blood of the cattle sacrificed in the riverbed served only to feed the ants. But Yidir now realizes that he and the late Bassu were not the only ones to fight against the drought, that in fact all the *qsar* dwellers prayed in the mosque, offered hundreds of candles to the saints and sacrificed many cattle on the burning sands of the Wad Tudgha – thus showing that even the most irrational solutions should not simply be discarded out of hand. His mother reminds him that with part of her inheritance she has bought a black heifer which she wants to sacrifice in order to exorcise Ittu's illness. Si Lahsin knows what must be done if the *jnun* inside her are Muslim, Yidir says, but in Ittu's case he can do nothing because the *jinn* which haunts her can only leave her if it is offered the hot sacrificial blood of a black cow.

So the heifer is prepared for sacrifice the next day, while Yidir and the *fqih* are not present. The sacrificial act takes place that same afternoon, performed by the local butcher, who offers the animal to Sidi Bu l-Man as well as to whoever is haunting the body of the young woman who is sitting, veiled, in front of it. Hadda dabs her daughter-in-law's forehead with a clot of coagulated calf's blood once the animal's head has been turned toward Mecca and its throat is cut – after which the meat is divided up among all those present, while the butcher keeps the head and the hide. Ittu is now reaccompanied home by the same procession which brought her out, and she must not speak to anyone until she has crossed the threshold of her husband's home, where she must now remain as a complete recluse for a full week without even seeing her children.

The *fqih* may think such a sacrifice of black cows to be heresy but Yidir is more tolerant. Before the week is up he goes in to see Ittu who is longing for him; but the formalities must be observed, at least outwardly. Yidir is aware that Ittu is now cured, especially after he pours some eau de cologne (which she adores because it smells like spring flowers) over her. So is Hadda, but the news must be kept quiet for a short while for propriety's sake, while the *qsar* dwellers are convinced that the cure of the young woman can only be explained by the sacrifice of the black heifer. Si Lahsin tells Yidir that in the last analysis it is God, of course, who cured his wife – but they then agree with each other that both of them believe fully in the sacrifice of good men who have shed their blood for their country.

On this note Layid's novel ends. The plot may be somewhat weak, but the ethnography is splendid. However, if, as noted earlier, my reactions to Khettouch and his 'good roots' are somewhat mixed, they are considerably more so with respect to Mahjoub Aherdan, *Un Poème pour Etendard* ('A Flag for a Poem', Aherdan 1991). This is a work of fiction, written in a kind of poetic prose, rather than a novel pure and simple, by a Berber from the Western Middle Atlas who also happens to be a figure of considerable political consequence in Morocco: a onetime member of his country's Army of Liberation against the French, later the founder of the *Haraka Sha'biya* or Popular Movement (MP), an essentially Berber political party, several times a cabinet minister, and, most recently, the Counsellor to the Throne. Indeed in quite a few respects, without being necessarily or even predominantly autobiographical, the book mirrors its author's early role in the resistance to French colonialism (ca. 1954-1955) and his subsequent climb to political eminence in the post-independence period, an eminence from which he has always been able to project a pro-Berber (and in particular, pro-Middle Atlas Imazighen) image without negating or even diminishing the other major ethnolinguistic image (i.e, the Arab one) which is the preponderant one in the country, to the tune of possibly 60%.

The work begins by stressing the legacy of the Imazighen past with which Muhammad u-Mhand and his wife Mayis inculcate their son Muh Idir from babyhood. It eventually becomes apparent that Muh Idir is the author himself under another name; and to this extent it is indeed autobiographical. But in my view (and I read the book twice to make sure), the defects of this work are considerable, a major one being that its main characters do not act, but only react, to external events both in their own tribe, the Iziyyan (or Zayyan), as the historical panorama unfolds from the alliance between Mawlay al-Hasan I (1873-94) and Muha u-Hammu on until Moroccan independence from France; and in this respect we get something approximating a wide-angle review in Aherdan. The French 'pacification' of the region, the 1914 victory of the Iziyyan at l-Hri and the subsequent Berber resistance in the Middle-Central Atlas are all given considerable play through the reactions to these events on the parts of those Iziyyan resident at Ulmas (Oulmes), of whom the author is a member. The thinly veiled description of his own youthful days at the French-sponsored *Collège Berbère* in Azru, for example, is of considerable interest. But as the author's own perception of the Berber past seems rather fuzzy, his perception of their future, at least in Morocco, is not a particularly rosy one. This is so even though he himself would probably be the first to admit that if their divisiveness was originally produced by the major Arab invasions after the eleventh century, their retention of this divisiveness is largely of their own making, and the result of having had a number of different ancestors common always to a minority but never to a majority.

The whole tenor of the book, too, is couched in legends at second hand as well as of discussion and dissection after the event. This is set down in the first section, 'Legacy', then strengthened in the second, 'Waves', laid down ironclad in the third, 'Vibrations', to lead on to the fourth, 'Fibers' and to the post-colonial fifth, 'Memory'. Now all of this might strike chords of awareness in the hearts of anthropologists of symbol-oriented and cognitivist tendencies, but there is precious little in it for those who were trained in structuralism: the net result of 250 pages' worth of this more or less psychically and allegorically oriented exploration of Middle Atlas Berber culture seems to me very thin indeed. The final admonition in the initial section, on 'Legacy', is that Amasmud, Asinhaj and Aznath, the three descendants of the founding father Amazigh, all paid attention to their great ancestor's words (ibid.: 35), while that of the last section, on 'Memory', is, in the very last line of the book, that the war cry of a resistant can also become a flag for a poem (ibid.: 251), thereby supposedly justifying the book's title. True enough, no doubt; but still rather trite.

The work is turgid, the main historical events (i.e., the betrayal of Mawlay Surur and the Battles of Tafudayt in 1913 and l-Hri in 1914) and personages (i.e., Muha u-Hammu) show no immediacy or urgency, and are always kept at at least one remove from the reader all the way. Aherdan seems also not to have discovered any happy medium (if one exists) between poetry and prose, both of which he insists on employing. In addition, not only is the ethnography (our main criterion of judgment and reference here) rather soggy, but ethnographic facts are often simply stated out of context, without any back-up or explanation, as though it should simply be accepted on faith. This does not even happen in Khettouch's work, much less in Layid's. What Aherdan's book reads like is what, in essence, it is: a running commentary, full of irrelevant flights of fancy, by the Iziyyan of Ulmas on what the real Iziyyan resistants of Khanifra and Agilmam Azigza did under Muha u-Hammu to resist French incursion into the Middle Atlas. It is true, of course, that the French were only thrown out by the succeeding generation, Aherdan's own. But it is very difficult to try to work out how all this happened in the area in question on the basis of this particular work.

The next novel to be considered is very different from all the others dealt with thus far, even though in at least one respect it picks up where Coon left off. It is essentially an assessment, in novelistic form, of the later role of Muhammad bin ᶜAbd al-Krim, the onetime leader of the Rifians in their war against both Spain and France (1921-26), in the general North African, but particularly Moroccan, nationalism in the 1950s, after jumping ship at Port Saᶜid in Egypt in 1947, at the invitation of King Faruq, while being transported, with his family, on a French steamer from a twenty-one year imprisonment on

Reunion Island to a more comfortable residence (though one to be still under surveillance) in France. The book in question is by a Spaniard, Fernando P. de Cambra, a novel disguised as a piece of investigative journalism and entitled *Cuando Abd el-Krim Quiso Negociar con Franco* ('When bin ᶜAbd al-Krim Wanted to Negotiate with Franco', de Cambra 1981). I should stress that it is indeed a novel, for it takes a great many liberties with history. It deals with a series of events which might have happened between 1954 and 1958 but which did not do so because political reasons from the top imposed a firmly unequivocal and unappealable negative, as de Cambra makes clear in his preface. Even so, despite numerous small errors as well as quite a few major ones, de Cambra's book is a good read. Much of what he says is plausible, even though it may not all have actually happened: for it has the ring of truth.

The story, which is told by its author in the first person (he is not afraid to use his own name, and he writes as if the novel were autobiographical) begins in Cairo in March 1954. De Cambra, a Spanish journalist (given the period, probably with *ABC* or *Ya*, although this is not specified) has returned to that city after nearly a two year absence. He has just met Nasser for the first time, who has suggested to him that he also arrange a meeting with the Amir Muhammad bin ᶜAbd al-Krim. At his very first interview with bin ᶜAbd al-Krim, in the latter's house, the old Rifian leader starts to speak with him in Spanish right away so that the Egyptian ministry official and photographer present will not understand; and he tells him that he wants to see him again soon, at dinner, and with no outsiders present. It is not until de Cambra's next trip back to Cairo after another news assignment that the dinner actually takes place.

Bin ᶜAbd al-Krim, in exile in Cairo since 1947, sees that the winds of independence are blowing hard in Morocco, and would like to do something to help hasten this objective. He knows that he is considered both a Grand Old Man and a prehistoric fossil by the younger North African nationalists, notably ᶜAllal al-Fasi. Nonetheless, hoping to use de Cambra as an intermediary, as they get on well and obviously like each other, bin Abd al-Krim has a proposition to put to Franco, which he wants de Cambra to take to the latter directly in Madrid, and without any other party to it, based on the idea that 'the enemies of yesterday can easily be friends today and even better friends tomorrow'. De Cambra then notes that only in 1975, right after Franco's death and twelve years after that of bin ᶜAbd al-Krim, has he dared to note any of this down.

Bin ᶜAbd al-Krim feels he owes nothing to France, as the French jailed him, humiliated him and deported him, whereas in Egypt he has been well treated ever since his arrival, and much old ground from the Rifian War of

1921-1926 is here recovered. What he wants to do is (according to de Cambra's novel) to return to the Rif, raise up his own Aith Waryaghar tribe and all their neighbors, reinvade the French zone of Morocco and put an end to the ʿAlawid dynasty (which is to say, Sultan Muhammad bin Yusuf, later King Muhammad v, and his son Crown Prince Hasan, later King Hasan II) once nationalist fervor has reached the point that the French have to pull out and that the Spanish have had to follow suit. His proposal to Franco is that during this period Spain maintain a benevolent neutrality after what will be, he hopes, a *fait accompli*, i.e., by turning a blind eye to his disembarkation, with suitable armament, on the Rifian coast. In return for this he would promise Spain undying friendship, most favored nation status and retention of all the Spanish *presidios* and the Western Sahara, even though the protectorate would have to go.

Such, in brief, is the proposal, as couched in mid-1954. But what with de Cambra going off on numerous journalistic assignments elsewhere, he does not get back to Madrid again until at least mid-1955, and probably not even until 1956 (de Cambra is very elastic about his dates, and those that do not suit his plot are ignored). At any rate, when Franco finally hears about the proposal, he turns it down flat, using old Spanish colonialist rhetoric about bin ʿAbd al-Krim being a 'traitor' (i.e., to Spain) and that therefore there is no question of making any deals with him – which, for Franco, would certainly have been in character.

Interestingly, however, the other side of the coin is that bin ʿAbd al-Krim equally wants the benevolent neutrality, if not the cooperation, of Hajj Tahami l-Glawi, who since 1951, at least, has detested the ʿAlawid dynasty as much as he does and who is also – and incidentally – a Berber-speaker, if not one from the same region (a point de Cambra, who also even speaks of the 'Arab' – sic(!) – 'Republic of the Rif', fails to mention). There follows an interesting and not totally implausible top secret interview between de Cambra and the Glawi which takes place in a tent, sometime in 1955, and somewhere off the main road between Bni Mallal (which de Cambra erroneously places in Algeria – his geography is at best hazy!) and l-Qalʿa Sraghna. The Glawi is cautiously optimistic, but adopts a 'wait-and-see' attitude, because by the summer of 1955, even despite his loyalty to France, he feels that the French will soon be so occupied by events in Algeria (for the Algerian Revolution broke out on November 1, 1954) that they will have to let Morocco and Tunisia go.

But everything is cut short by the return of King Muhammad v from exile in Madagascar in November of the same year and by his humiliation and dismissal of the Glawi which resulted in the latter's subsequent death in January 1956. In a later, post-independence scene (about 1957) in Munich, however, the late Idris al-Khattabi, bin ʿAbd al-Krim's youngest son (who was, in fact, born during his father's exile on Reunion Island and killed in Casablanca in July-August 1980 in an automobile accident), says his father now wants no more to do with Franco but would like de Cambra, who is also a boating and yachting enthusiast, to skipper the boat delivering the hoped-for arms shipment to a point, as yet unspecified, on the Rifian coast. De Cambra, however, after due consideration, refuses, wisely, to take the job on because the chances of its success are so infinitesimal. Here the book ends, with the chronicling, in its conclusion, of the deaths of most of its principals within the next few years, into the 1960s and 1970s.

Nothing is said in de Cambra's book, however, about either the activities of the Moroccan Army of Liberation in the Rif from October 1955 through June 1956, or about the very serious Aith Waryaghar uprising against the Moroccan government from October 1958 through January 1959; yet these crucial events would certainly have been grist for de Cambra's mill. Also, de Cambra has, as noted, an unfortunate tendency to juggle his dates or to ignore them completely, such as the independence of the Spanish protectorate which he says, very wrongly, came only through a separate treaty in April 1957, whereas in fact it occurred in April 1956, a year earlier, only a month after the independence of the French zone. His treatment of bin ʿAbd al-Krim is certainly sympathetic, but he obviously knows nothing of the Rif, the region that produced him. He is also obviously no friend of the ʿAlawid dynasty, of Kings Muhammad V and his son Hasan II, such that if, as must surely be the case, his book was banned in Morocco, the reason is not far to seek. For that matter, a further question that might be asked (quite apart from the rather flimsy character of bin ʿAbd al-Krim's secret proposal to Franco) is: what really is there on record with respect to bin ʿAbd al-Krim's own actual reactions to the ʿAlawids? Only the fact that he never evidently accepted or even answered the invitation of King Muhammad V to return to Morocco either before the latter's sudden death in Rabat in March 1961 or his own in Cairo in February 1963, while his younger brother Si Mhammad did so in 1967 but died the same year shortly after reaching Casablanca, and without ever seeing the Rif again. Finally, de Cambra's novel is heavily padded with extraneous details, such as flights around the Arab Mediterranean on reportorial assignments, contacts with Arab nationalists and political figures, and with agents of the intelligence services of most of the countries involved politically in the region. These have really very little to do with the main thread of bin ʿAbd al-Krim's proposal to Franco and the latter's rejection of it. These two events, although they never happened, nonetheless remain plausible and make for a good story — although it might have better yet as a long short story than as an overly padded novel of 281 pages. (For a synopsis of bin ʿAbd al-Krim's career after he lost the Rifian War, and of events in the Rif since 1926, cf. Hart 1976: 405-436).

Finally, I consider briefly at two novels by another Moroccan writer, Driss Chraibi. The first, *Une Enquête au Pays* ('An Investigation in the Country', Chraibi 1981) is a savagely amusing story about a Moroccan police chief in Casablanca, Muhammad, and his inspector subordinate ʿAli, who are detailed to go up into the Ait Yafalman country in the Eastern Atlas (although the location is never truly specified) in order to track down and arrest a criminal. Their own semi-Westernized ideas about traditional Moroccan Muslim society, about colonialism and about galloping sociocultural change in the cities are all lampooned, as are the semi-French neologisms in which they express them (i.e., '*les insectuels*' for 'intellectuals'). This is particularly the case with Chief Muhammad, who wants always to go by the book. And this particular book is both the poetic and ironic reflection on how best to resist creeping mental retardation by the bureaucracy and the 'big wheels' ('*les grosses huiles*'), and how to save the luminous peace of hearts and minds, as the commentary on the back cover by Bernard Poirot-Delpech of *Le Monde* has noted. Some of it is far-fetched, although the emphasis on a traditional Islamic 'timelessness' as shown by the behavior of the members of the Ait Yafalman community (Rahu and Hajja) is obviously intended as a counterbalance to the imbecility of the two policemen. However, the fact that Rahu was once a commandant in the Algerian (not Moroccan) National Army of Liberation (ALN) is hard to swallow, as is the fact that the village idiot Basfaw, who proves to be the 'real' criminal, was also evidently formerly a labor migrant in that country. This is curious, as the real Ait Yafalman are a Berber tribal confederacy with no tradition whatsoever of labor migration. At any rate the moronic police chief is quietly done away with and the inspector comes back a year later as chief himself, with a new inspector in tow, to find that all the villagers have departed. The blurb in the inside cover, obviously written by Chraibi himself, is an amusing castigation of Chraibi's own work by Inspector ʿAli, and it reads like a Moroccan police dossier spelled out in less than totally correct French administrative jargon.

The second novel by Chraibi to be considered here, *La Mère du Printemps (L'Oum er-Rbia)* ('The Mother of Spring', *Umm ar-Rbi$^c$*, Chraibi 1982) is named for one of Morocco's major rivers, and the action takes us back to the beginnings of Islam in the country. The same Berber villagers who appeared in *Une Enquête au Pays* are also present in the long epilogue at the beginning (!) of the book; and hence it is quite possible that they also appear in some of Chraibi's other novels as well. However, this one goes back to the arrival of the Arab general and conqueror ʿUqba bin Nafiʿ at the mouth of the Umm ar-Rbiʿ or 'Mother of Spring' river, at what was much later to become the town of Azimmur, on the Moroccan Atlantic coast, in 681 CE. The Ait Yafalman tribe (*ait yafalman* is incorrectly translated by Chraibi as 'sons of water' when its real meaning is 'those who want peace') under their *amghar* Azwaw are awaiting the arrival of the Arab invaders. They are plagued by the dilemma of what to do if resistance should prove useless and of how to remain true to themselves during the process of change. (The work is, significantly, dedicated to all the minorities of the world which, taken, together, constitute its vast majority; and it may also be of some significance to point out that Chraibi himself is an 'Arab' from Azimmur who is not at all 'anti-Berber'...)

In any event, on the advice of a sage, the Jew Azulay, the Berber Azwaw gives his son the Arabic name of Yasin, for he realizes that the new religious 'password' may be *Allahu Akbar*. Azwaw leads the assembly in saying that the Berbers of the Ait Yafalman will not resist the Arabs in any way except possibly in terms of time, simply because weeds invariably win out against good grass. As the Arab conquerors enter the Berbers, so will the Berbers, in time, enter the Arabs. Azwaw then leads the rest of his tribe in taking an oath to this effect, in 679, after which he nearly drowns in the sacred waters of the Umm ar-Rbiʿ. After this he sends members of his tribe out to settle down in all parts of the Maghrib, while waiting for ʿUqba. When the latter arrives, Azwaw's wife Hineb is killed, but the name of Yasin, a *sura* or chapter of the Qur'an, stops all further killing while ʿUqba and Azwaw have a close look at each other. The former is convinced that the latter is not yet a Muslim but that he will become one and that his son Yasin will spread the word of Allah. The Imam Filani, it is added, the man who originally recorded this tale, was himself once an u-Yafalman; and the book ends on the note that all the Ait Yafalman embraced Islam by entering into their conquerors. It also seems a fitting note on which to terminate this disquisition on works of fiction about Moroccan Muslim tribesmen.

# FILMS

With respect to those films, admittedly few in number, dealing with Muslim tribesmen and the colonial encounter which I consider to be worthy of sustained comment, an initial, and quite general, caveat must be made with respect to economic, social and/or political change in any country or region where the original scenario of the film took place. It is this: that oftener than not, owing to the very fact of such change, any film dealing with events that happened half a century or more ago cannot be made 'on location', so to speak, simply because of the very great changes, during the interim, in the location itself. A suitable substitute must therefore generally, and quite legitimately, be looked for or be 'on tap'; and it must be one which conforms visually, to a greater or lesser degree, to the environmental conditions prescribed by the original locality of the action. These ecological demands have been met by filmmakers with varying degrees of success: 'Memed My Hawk' (1978), for example, based on Yashar Kemal's excellent novel already commented upon, is in itself a fine film but the fact that it was made in Yugoslavia rather than in Anatolia where the events in question happened (in the backcountry above Adana) may have provided splendid mountain scenery but detracted from the overall reality of the production, as the far more denuded landscape of south-central Anatolia would have given us the clinching element of authenticity, of *Echtheit*.

I begin my film analysis with the joint production, virtually flawless in my view, by David Lean and Sam C. Spiegel of 'Lawrence of Arabia', both in its original 1962 version, as in the later uncut one of 1990. The cast, including Peter O'Toole in the title role, Omar Sharif, Alec Guinness, Anthony Quinn, Anthony Quayle, Jack Hawkins, Arthur Kennedy, Claude Rains and José Ferrer, is uniformly excellent: everyone does a splendid job. But the real prize, if a single one can be awarded, should perhaps go to Robert Bolt for his truly superlative screenplay. However, not one iota of this film was shot in Arabia, properly speaking; and indeed very little of the historical action of T.E. Lawrence (1888-1935) and his organization of the Arab Revolt against the Ottoman Turks during World War I (1916-18) took place there either, but in points further to the northwest. Only insofar as the Hijaz was concerned was what is today Saudi Arabia involved. Large tracts of the film were made in southern Morocco (my wife and I happened to be doing fieldwork in the Warzazat province when some of the scenes were shot, with Moroccan extras taking the parts of Turkish soldiers), while others were filmed in Jordan, which did indeed account for a good part of the action. The rest was filmed in that onetime filmland Mecca, the Almeria province of southeastern Spain, with Almeria itself doubling as Cairo in 1916-18 and the port of Carboneras, suitably mocked up, acting as that of ᶜAqaba during the same period: for it is obvious that neither ᶜAqaba nor Carboneras today bears much resemblance to the ᶜAqaba that was guarded in World War I by 12-inch Turkish guns looking out to sea and which was attacked by Lawrence, Sharif ᶜAli (Omar Sharif) and ᶜAwda Abu Tayyiᶜ (Anthony Quinn) from the rear after a brutal traversing on camelback of the Nafud Desert.

The film's prologue shows Lawrence's accidental death in 1935, when, on a motorcycle, he skidded and crashed off a country road in England to avoid hitting two small boys on bicycles. Then comes the flashback to the Near East during World War I. The taking of ᶜAqaba from the Ottoman Turks in 1916 by Lawrence and his Bedouin irregulars after a long, hard forced march on camelback across the desert provides the first climax of the film, but what leads up to it is also of interest. A British 'Colonel Blimp' military man in Cairo typically places no confidence at all in the military value of Bedouins and sees any combat between them and Turkish troops as 'a sideshow of a sideshow', while the 'real' war is being fought in the trenches in France against the Germans. When Lawrence's first Bedouin guide from the Bani Salim is shot by Sharif ᶜAli of the Harith for stealing water from his well, on their way to the camp of the Amir Faysal, Lawrence tells ᶜAli that as long as one Arab tribe fights against another, the Arabs will remain a puny little people. After Faysal's camp is bombed and machine-gunned by two Turkish planes, Faysal (Alec Guinness) longs for the vanished gardens of Cordoba and the glories of the Arabo-Muslim past; but he admits that the Arabs must fight to regain them.

It is then that Lawrence gets his brainstorm about taking ᶜAqaba by land rather than by sea; and the whole sequence of the march on ᶜAqaba in blazing desert heat is nothing if not dramatic. It is interrupted only by the meeting of Lawrence's and ᶜAli's force with ᶜAwda Abu Tayyiᶜ, who accuses Lawrence's raiding party of stealing his water. However, he invites them all to dinner, and says, musingly, that of course the Huwaytat are his own tribe, that he knows all about the Bani Sakhr, the Harb and even (looking at ꜥAli) the Harith – but he then asks, 'But who are these "Arabs"?' He pleads poverty for having dispensed so much hospitality, and then confides to Lawrence that the Turks pay him a retainer of 100 golden guineas a month. To this Lawrence replies that he knows it to be 150, and still a mere trifle, and that the Turks are giving ꜥAwda the short end of the stick. So ꜥAwda joins them on the march to ꜥAqaba, and they are seen off to the ululations of the women. On the way, one of Lawrence's men, Qasim, whom he has just saved from death by sunstroke, then murders a Huwayti with whom he is at feud; and he must die, Lawrence as a neutral opts to kill him (after which he throws his pistol away and a flurry of Bedouins rush to pick it up).

After ꜥAqaba is taken, ꜥAwda is annoyed not to find any gold there, so Lawrence writes out an IOU for 5,000 golden guineas and promises to be back in ten days with the money and many more arms. He now crosses the Sinai peninsula and desert to get back to Cairo, where he tells an astonished Gen. Allenby (Jack Hawkins) how he captured ꜥAqaba, and is able to obtain a promise from him of more money and arms for the Bedouins forthwith. On his return, he is interviewed by a 'Mr. Bentley' (in reality Lowell Thomas, well played by Arthur Kennedy) of the *Chicago Tribune*, who then watches him and his Bedouins dynamite, capture and loot a Turkish train. At the end of this exploit Lawrence is shot in the shoulder by a wounded Turkish officer, who is then decapitated by ꜥAwda with a sword. The latter is disgusted with the grandfather clock he gets as booty, but is pleased on finding a splendid stallion on board when they raid the next train. ꜥAwda is now ready to go home, with his men, while a shocked Col. Brighton (Anthony Quayle) calls him a deserter and a cad, to which his retort is that the latter's behavior is as stupid and as piggish as his face.

Lawrence has promised Allenby and the Cairo high command that he will take the Arab revolt to the Turks and to this end he reconnoiters the Turkish garrison town of Daraꜥa, where is interviewed by a sadistic and obviously homosexual Turkish colonel (José Ferrer) who has him tortured. By this time Allenby has occupied Jerusalem, where he and Lawrence now have a major personality clash. Lawrence wants to resign from the army but after Allenby tells him about the Sykes-Picot agreement – of which he was evidently totally unaware – between Britain and France to parcel out the Ottoman empire between them after the war is over, he tells Allenby that he will give the Arabs Damascus. On his way there with a 2,000-man irregular Bedouin cavalry/camelry force, they charge an escaping Turkish column after resolving to take no prisoners, and Lawrence himself, who has found earlier on that he enjoys killing (and may also possibly have enjoyed the Turkish colonel's sadomasochism), shoots down one Turkish soldier after another, until ʿAli tells him to desist. By the time Allenby reaches Damascus, Lawrence's Bedouins have already been there two days and, always at odds with each other, have, to the sound of gunshots, occupied the town hall for a 'conference' of the 'Arab National Council', which is in a perpetual uproar from beginning to end; and the end is brought about only because of a power cut. A cut of another kind then moves us to the few remaining Turkish prisoners, whose treatment by the Bedouins the British regard as 'outrageous', after the 'conference' has broken up with nothing achieved. At this point a Mr. Dryden of the British Foreign Office (Claude Rains), the 'architect of the Sykes-Picot compromise', confesses to wishing that he had stayed in Tunbridge Wells (an observation which may be contrasted with one by Lawrence himself, who when asked by the American correspondent why he liked the desert, replied, romantically, 'Because it's clean!'). In the final scene a Cockney driver escorts a very disgruntled Lawrence in a staff car, passing lines of returning Bedouins, and reminds him, 'Ain't it noice to be goin' 'ome, sir?' It took all types, it would seem, to produce the colonialist mentality, and Lawrence, Allenby and Dryden were only three of them.

There is, to be sure, a great deal in this wonderful film for the devotees of T.E. Lawrence himself, but even more for those of us who know, have worked with and like Arab Bedouins. The same cannot be said either for the two Alexander Korda productions of 'The Drum' (1938), filmed on the Pakistan (then Indian) North-West Frontier, and 'Four Feathers' (1939), about the British 'reconquest' of the Sudan under Kitchener and the destruction of the Mahdist army at Umm Durman in 1898, any more than for the Julian Blaustein production of 'Khartoum' (1964), dealing with the earlier period of Sudanese Mahdism, with Charlton Heston as an overly nonchalant Gen. Gordon and Laurence Olivier as a totally uncomprehending Sudanese Mahdi. Between the two of them Heston and Olivier gave the most wooden performances it has ever been my misfortune to see, and this despite the fact that the film was obviously made on location in Sudan, as was the earlier Korda production, and despite the splendid performances of all the Sudanese extras, who were obviously enjoying themselves (especially at the best scene, the massacre by the Mahdists, early on, of Gen. Hicks' column in 1883). However, the depiction of Gordon's statue in Khartum but the omission of the Mahdi's shrine across the Nile in Umm Durman at the end of the film I regard as a colonialistic *faux pas* of the first order – particularly in a film produced well into the post-colonial period.

There is not much to be said either for two films about Afghanistan, 'The Horsemen' (1970) and 'Caravans' (1972), the former based on a very bad novel by Joseph Kessel and the latter on a somewhat better one by James Michener (1965); but it is one which I would still regard as essentially unworthy of comment here, mainly because of its insufficient ethnographic value. In 'The Horsemen', Omar Sharif, who looks the Egyptian that he is, is miscast as a Turkoman (or Turkic) *chapandaz* horseman, the captain of a *buzkashi* team, especially as he does not look like a Tatar. (Buzkashi is the Afghan national game, invented by Turkic-speaking nomads in the north of the country and played by two teams on horseback, each of which tries to capture a goat or a calf from the other: cf. Dupree 1980: 218-21; Azoy 1982). In 'Caravans', Anthony Quinn, once again, takes the role of the Ghilzai nomad tribal khan and does so effectively, but the plot and sometimes even the action founder because the notion of 'tribe' is imperfectly understood and the thorny question of tribe-state relations even less so. Quinn as the chief makes the mistake (carried over from Michener's book, and quite normal for a layman) of saying that nomads own nothing that they cannot carry; but he does not think to mention their tribal *watan* or *dira*, their territory, which is theirs alone. The film was made, as it happens, in the Qashqa'i country of southern (and pre-revolutionary) Iran, although the nomad tribesmen depicted are not Qashqa'i at all, but Ghilzai Pukhtuns from Afghanistan.

'The Wind and the Lion' (1975), starring Sean Connery, Candice Bergen, Brian Keith and John Huston, and directed by John Milius, is more than anything else a bad historical joke, albeit with one or two good moments. It purports to describe an episode in Moroccan-US relations at the beginning of the twentieth century, the kidnapping, just outside Tangier, of an allegedly American citizen, Ion Perdicaris, in May 1904 (although the film gives the date erroneously as October 15 of the same year) by a northern Moroccan *sharif*-turned-bandit, Mawlay Ahmad al-Raysuni, and its aftermath, which produced the famous telegram from a reelection-seeking president, Theodore Roosevelt, which read 'Perdicaris Alive or Raysuni Dead'. This was followed up by a display of gunboat diplomacy in Tangier harbor, although Raysuni himself was able to milk a ransom of 70,000 dollars out of Roosevelt (cf. Tuchman 1984 for the episode itself; and Forbes 1924 and Hart 1976: 390-93, as well as Hart 1987: 19-26, for biographical information on Raysuni). The film's initial error with respect to the date is greatly compounded throughout the whole two and a half hours' running time. The attack on the Perdicaris household, and the killing of an unidentified male houseguest, is carried out by men dressed as blue-robed Western Saharans, or even as Algerians, on horseback, instead of by local Moroccan Jbala tribesmen in brown knee-length *jillabas* and white turbans, on foot. Sean Connery, who takes the part of Raysuni, is the leader of this motley crew, and indeed, when my wife and I took our Moroccan maid, from Marrakesh, to see the film, she asked me in Arabic who their Saharan leader was and if he were working for the Polisario Front! Connery as Raysuni, in his blue-black Saharan-style robes, exudes a romantic image in the film which the real Raysuni, in his own pragmatic and highly bet-hedging life style, could not have had at all; and Connery's frequent and mechanical recitation in the film of Raysuni's pedigree indicates a lack of understanding of the function of a *sharif*-ly genealogy in Moroccan Islam (for, as noted, a *sharif* is a descendant of the Prophet, and Morocco is loaded with them), because it comes out sounding like a joke instead of the virtual guarantee of saintly status that it is in fact. 'I am Mawlay Ahmad bin Muhammad al-Raysuni, the Magnificent, Lord of the Rif and Sultan of the Berbers', indeed: Raysuni was neither a Rifian nor a Berber of any sort, but he was certainly to meet his come-uppance at the hands of one, Muhammad bin ᶜAbd al-Krim al-Khattabi, just twenty years after the events described in this film (Hart 1976, 1987). To top it all, Perdicaris himself is substituted by Mrs. Perdicaris (Candice Bergen), who, although she certainly existed in real life, played no role in the kidnapping. Obviously the director, John Milius, figured that the film had to have a 'love interest', and this is precisely the role that Mrs. Perdicaris plays.

Closer to the mark, perhaps, Teddy Roosevelt (Brian Keith) is also something of a joke and his outraged attitudes toward Raysuni are another. In the film, of course, he himself formulates the famous telegram, whereas in fact the idea was dreamed up by his Secretary of State, John Hay (John Huston), as a vote-getting gesture for Roosevelt in the upcoming Republican Party nomination as candidate for president, as well as an indicator of the growing status of the US as a fledgling world power on the international scene. However, the film plays down or even avoids entirely the fact that Perdicaris himself, who had a Greek father but an American mother and who was born in America, went back to Greece about 1860 and took out Greek citizenship, possibly to avoid conscription in the Union Army during the American Civil War!

With respect to Raysuni, however, it is of course quite true that he emerged at a very troubled period in Moroccan history, during the decade or more just before the implantation of Franco-Spanish colonial rule when the country was itself in the throes of a *de facto* civil war. But Connery as Raysuni sums it up with trite aphorisms along the lines of 'With the Sultan (Mawlay ᶜAbd al-ᶜAziz) a prisoner of his European advisors, it is up to me to rally his men to fight the Europeans', when in fact his guiding principle was always, first and foremost, to be on the lookout for No. 1; and the meeting and greeting between the 'Lord of the Rif' and the 'Lord of the Desert', which was totally fictitious, can be more realistically viewed as an exchange between two horsetraders, who both look Algerian because of the way their turbans are tied. Even so, Raysuni rightly finds Roosevelt's telegram offensive, while Moroccan Arabic is actually spoken by quite a few of the extras, such as the thieves in Raysuni's garden who implore him, in vain, to spare their lives before he beheads them.

One good and most amusing touch is provided by the young Moroccan actor who plays the Sultan Mawlay ᶜAbd al-ᶜAziz: he is fascinated by European gadgetry, plays bicycle polo, practices firing a machine-gun that runs away with him, and climbs up on a black slave's bent back to get into his royal carriage. His assessment of his classificatory 'uncle' Raysuni as a great man and descendant of the Prophet but also as a bandit and a criminal is not far removed from that of modern and postcolonial Moroccan historians, who look on him as just one of a number of immediately precolonial warlords (albeit a very successful one), and in no sense as a nationalist or as a hero of the resistance, as is the case with bin ᶜAbd al-Krim.

Parts of this film were made in southeastern Spain, as Almeria substitutes for Tangier on occasion and the very Christian round-towered fortress of La Calahorra in the northern foothills of the Sierra Nevada is mistakenly made up to represent a Muslim square-towered one in Morocco. But the biggest error of all is still to come: it is the introduction of Imperial Germany into the scenario, on a front-and-center basis. (It is true that Kaiser Wilhelm II visited Tangier in 1905, but the visit was part of an unsuccessful bid to contest the enormously increasing French influence in the country, which never even gets a mention in the film, while that of the Germans is swollen out of all proportion to reality.) So, in the film, Mawlay ᶜAbd al-ᶜAziz comes to favor the German Kaiser while his classificatory cousin the pasha of Tangier (with whom Raysuni is bitterly at feud – this much at least is correct!) favors the Russian Tsar. Hence the USA decides on military intervention, i.e., to 'send in the marines'. One gets the feeling that Milius, departing completely from the script of history, wanted to bring on World War I a decade before it actually started. We are also never informed as to the identity of a rival bandit gang, also dressed in Saharan robes, who are all defeated and killed by Raysuni on the Atlantic beach by the Caves of Hercules. From here on in the action goes totally haywire: two companies of US Marines, quick-marching with fixed bayonets, move in to fire point blank at the Tangier pasha's guardsmen and to capture the pasha himself, while in Washington Theodore Roosevelt takes pot shots at targets made up of the Kaiser and the Tsar, although he admits that J. Pierpont Morgan is a bigger bandit than Raysuni. He then offers Raysuni 70,000 dollars to release Mrs. Perdicaris and her children (who have in fact much enjoyed Raysuni's company); but with magisterial Hollywood disregard for history, the German legation troops trap them and take Raysuni prisoner when he is betrayed by the 'Lord of the Desert'. Mrs. Perdicaris then frees him, with the help of the marines, such that a German-American incident begins and ends in Raysuni's, 'The Lion's', triumph in the interior while Teddy 'The Wind' Roosevelt is still blowing hard with his gunboats on the coast. The film is claptrap, but it would have been better claptrap had it been a total fabrication. Unfortunately it contains a few grains of truth – though no more than this; and they were unable even to get the dates right.

The two final films in my purview are both directed by the Syrian Moustapha Akkad (Mustafa ᶜAqqad), and are of very high quality indeed. The first of them, 'The Message' (al-Risala; or 'Muhammad, the Messenger of God', 1976), is a British-Kuwaiti co-production, featuring Anthony Quinn, Irene Papas and Michael Ansara, with screenplay by H.A.L. Craig. It is no less than a film biography of the Prophet Muhammad, and was approved both by al-Azhar University in Cairo and by the Shiᶜa Council of Lebanon, while the Egyptian novelist Tawfiq al-Hakim figures among the members of its advisory board. The film's credentials are therefore highly respectable, and a notice is posted at the outset saying that out of respect for Islamic tradition and for the Muslim ban on the representation of human figures, the person of the Prophet is never shown. The filming was done almost entirely in Morocco and in Libya. (For worthwhile biographies of the Prophet by Western scholars, cf. Watt 1961 and Rodinson 1976.)

In the opening scene, emissaries of the new religion, Islam, are sent from Arabia to Egypt, Byzantium and Persia to see if their rulers will accept the new faith; and the satrap of Persia tears up the scroll presented to him. We then move back to Mecca in 610 CE, where Muhammad bin ᶜAbdallah, the Messenger-to-be, is in the cave at al-Hira' where he hears the voice of the Angel Jibril (Gabriel) commanding him 'Read – in the name of the Lord, who created man from a germ-cell...' (Qur'an, Sura 96). To this Muhammad replies that he cannot read, that he is illiterate, to which Jibril insists that he read, telling him who he is and that he, Muhammad, is the Messenger of God. Muhammad tells (or rather, it comes out that he has told) his wife Khadija, his cousin ⁽Ali and his uncle Abu Talib of his revelation – and they become his first followers. The wealthy and powerful Meccan animist Abu Sufyan, and his daughter Hind (Irene Papas), order their black slave Bilal to whip ⁽Ali, who persists in following Muhammad; but he refuses, and is whipped himself by Abu Sufyan's son Umayya, while proclaiming that there is only one God, not three hundred minor deities. Bilal then performs the very first Muslim call to prayer from the Ka⁽ba in Mecca, when the rest of the Quraysh (Muhammad's tribe) start to stone and to fight the Muslims, who have now grown to about thirty in number. Then the warrior Hamza (Anthony Quinn) appears to back up his nephew Muhammad's claim to revelation of a new faith. But after an initial battle with the Meccans he urges them to leave for Ethiopia, where the Lion of Judah, on hearing the evidence from both sides, will not turn over the fledgling Muslim community to the heathen Meccans. The latter now kick the Muslims out of town completely, and the new Muslim community falls on hard times when, first, Muhammad's wife Khadija dies and then his uncle Abu Talib does, both as converts to Islam.

A delegation now comes from Medina to the north to ask the Muslims to arbitrate between two rival factions there. They agree to do so if the latter will accept the fact that there is only one God, Allah. And so we come to 622 CE and the *hijra* or exodus of the Muslims, now seventy people, to Medina – an exodus which changed the world. Muhammad himself is the last to migrate; and even so he is pursued by his enemies. A spider weaving its web across the mouth of a cave and a dove nesting inside the cave itself both help him to escape his would-be killers and to get to Medina. Wherever his she-camel stops is where he will build his house. Thus the first mosque is built and the black ex-slave Bilal, chosen for his strong and resonant voice (and well played in the film), calls the first prayer from it. When Hamza learns that the Meccans have despoiled all the property that the escaping Muslims left behind on making their *hijra*, he wants to fight them, with the help of the Medinese *ansar*, the new converts and companions of the Prophet. The Battle of Badr ensues: first Hamza, ⁽Ali and another Muslim champion slay the three Meccan champions sent against them, after which the battle begins in earnest; and Bilal kills Umayya bin Abi Sufyan for having whipped and insulted him.

A good touch is that the Meccans are always more richly dressed than the Muslims, and display jewelry and bright colors, while the Muslims are entirely in white (save for Hamza's black 'Saharan-style' turban). The localities where the filming was done reveal themselves through the southern Moroccan *qsur* and through the *bandir* tambourine music, to say nothing of the very Berber faces of many of the extras. The Ethiopian slave Wahshi, working for the Meccans, is a kind of counterweight to Bilal; and as he is very dexterous at spear-throwing, Hind wants him to kill Hamza in return for his weight in silver. And so a 3,000-man Meccan army comes to Uhud to get revenge for the defeat at Badr. Wahshi kills Hamza, and Hind eats part of his heart, as he had previously killed both her father and her brother. After the battle the Muslims say that God sent them their defeat in order to test their faith, and that their own dead are in paradise and the Meccan dead in hell.

A ten-year truce is then decreed, and ʿUmar ibn al-Khattab, Khalid ibn al-Walid and ʿAmr ibn al-As all convert to Islam. But the Meccans break the truce, so Muhammad and the Muslims now come back to Mecca in triumph. They proceed to smash all the false idols in the Kaʿba, and Bilal once more climbs up on top of it to call the prayer of Islam to a now much wider and very much more receptive audience. Muhammad then declares (or it is so reported) that everything in Mecca must now be kept sacrosanct. The film ends with the circumambulation of a few dozen Muslims around the Kaʿba, which then magnifies into the hundreds, thousands and millions that do so during the course of performing the rites of the *hajj* today. Muhammad dies at 63 in 632 CE, but his message lives on, and the recitation of the *shahada*, the Muslim profession of faith, is combined with the final commentary on the *hajj*. The last shots are particularly effective, of the *shahada* being intoned from minarets in mosques all over the Muslim world: a better and more graphic way of showing the essential brotherhood of the *umma* or Muslim community could not have been devised. And the last words spoken in the film are *al-salam ʿalaykum*, 'peace be upon you', the traditional greeting of one Muslim to another. We ourselves regard this production as an exceptionally good and effective one.

Also very good, but harking back again to the colonial scene early in the twentieth century is 'The Lion of the Desert' (or 'Omar El Mukhtar', 1981), also directed by Moustapha Akkad, and filmed both in Italy (where it was subsequently banned) and in Libya, with Anthony Quinn, once again, as ʿUmar al-Mukhtar, who headed the Cyrenaican Bedouin resistance to Italian colonization, Rod Steiger as Mussolini and Oliver Reed as Marshal Graziani, all of whom turn in splendid performances. Although the fact is nowhere indicated in the credit lines, the cost of this excellent film was borne probably singlehandedly by Col. Muʿammar al-Qaddafi of Libya, and as we shall soon see, in certainly one glaring respect it carries the Libyan colonel's revision of his country's history. The beginning is a study of contemporary photographs of the initial Italian occupation of Libya in 1911, both via Tripoli and via

Banghazi. Shortly thereafter Bedouin resistance to the invaders begins, and by 1922, when Mussolini comes to power, he does his best to keep Italian colonization up financially and in other ways by hanging Bedouin tribal leaders. By 1929 there are many more Italian executions of Libyan Bedouin prisoners, and Mussolini wants nothing short of total victory.

Mussolini therefore sends Gen. Rodolfo Graziani over to crush the elusive Bedouins once and for all, in particular their leader, an old *shaykh* named ʿUmar al-Mukhtar. Interestingly and significantly, however, there is no mention anywhere (except maybe once in passing) of the Sanusiya *tariqa* or religious order, which during this whole period worked more or less in tandem with the Bedouins to keep anti-Italian resistance alive and functioning (cf. Evans-Pritchard 1949, 1954, 1971). The Sanusiya are completely omitted, and very purposely so, because Col. Qaddafi, who brought their regime to an end by toppling King Idris al-Sanusi in 1969, obviously wanted them obliterated from history after having overthrown them. So for this reason we are, in effect, presented with only half the story of the Libyan resistance, as the other, Sanusi, side of the coin is entirely missing. Nonetheless, such is (or would have been) hardly Mussolini's concern: in no way will he permit a handful of Bedouins to impede the progress of forty million Italians!

Once the historical photos are shown, there is a very good live opening scene in which ʿUmar al-Mukhtar is teaching the village boys the Qur'an, when a wedding procession comes along to break up the lesson. However, it should be noted that the liberties allowed to Bedouin women with respect to veiling, seclusion, etc., reflect more the situation of 1981 than that of 1929, when it was supposed to have taken place. ʿUmar al-Mukhtar, on hearing of the arrival of Graziani, the 'Butcher of the Fezzan', takes on a new offensive command; and his viewpoint is interestingly contrasted with the collaborationist (or *bani oui-oui*) stance of the pasha of Banghazi (played by John Gielgud). Next we witness a wholesale torching by the Italians of Bedouin settlements and grain supplies, along with indiscriminate shooting of civilians; and this is just a foretaste of what is to happen under Graziani. In one village, the *shaykh* spits in the face of the Italian commanding officer, who then slaps him, shoots him down and starts a wholesale massacre just to set an example. But later the same Italian column is decimated in the desert, and ʿUmar al-Mukhtar returns a captured Italian flag to a lieutenant, saying, 'Tell your general that this flag is not ours.' The ensuing total war waged by the Italians against an innocent and almost defenseless people is very tellingly portrayed, as is the indomitable spirit of ʿUmar al-Mukhtar, especially when the Italians start to machine-gun Bedouins from armored cars.

An even worse initiative is taken when Graziani starts to put Bedouin prisoners into barbed wire camps. A 'peace talk' or parley comes up next, at which ʿUmar al-Mukhtar voices his desire for a Bedouin (or a Libyan) parliament. But Rome does not intend to give them one iota of autonomy, and wants all Bedouin land for colonization. Hence the talks end in total failure; and indeed one wonders if or why they ever took place at all. Graziani now marches with tanks and armored cars toward Kufra while ʿUmar al-Mukhtar intends to attack the Italians in the north. (As no coordination between the Bedouins and the Sanusiya order is even mentioned, one wonders if the Libyan resistance was organized to this extent, and indeed just how it kept going as long as it did. But Qaddafi, who paid for the film, also banned Evans-Pritchard's book on the Sanusi from Libya (Evans-Pritchard 1971)). While Italian planes bomb the Kufra oasis, *musabilin* sharpshooters, each with one leg tied up so that he will not abandon his post, are crushed to death in the desert by Italian tank treads rolling over the dunes, and mass executions are accompanied to the strains of 'La Giovanezza'. The hanging of Bedouin prisoners in the Italian concentration camps while all the others are made to watch is particularly horrifying.

Now in the Jabal al-Akhdar or 'Green Mountain' of Cyrenaica, ʿUmar al-Mukhtar says that the Italian capture of Kufra has closed the south to him. Despite the obvious authenticity of the Jabal al-Akhdar scenery (which looks to us remarkably like the Algerian Aures, at least on film), the roads, bridges, etc., in the region look much more like vintage 1980 than like 1930, although all the cars have a British 1930s look. Particularly revolting is Graziani's chortle of laughter after his forces bomb out Bedouin inhabited caves. But then ʿUmar al-Mukhtar stages a final splendid ambush of Italian tanks. Graziani wants to finish the resistance by planting barbed wire entanglements everywhere. However, it is gratifying that one particularly nasty Italian officer gets his just desserts when a nearly dead Bedouin on the battlefield leaps up and knifes him. In a retreat from this scene, ʿUmar al-Mukhtar's horse is hit, and he falls off both dazed and slightly wounded. He is captured, clapped in irons and taken prisoner. Only one single Italian officer (Raf Vallone) voices the view that as a valiant enemy of twenty years' standing ʿUmar al-Mukhtar should be treated with respect, an appeal which falls on totally deaf ears. It might be noted, however, that Anthony Quinn, in the role of ʿUmar, performs his ablutions prior to prayer in jail very nicely. The summing up of the whole film is contained in the short discourse between ʿUmar al-Mukhtar and Graziani and in ʿUmar's complete refusal to collaborate in any way with the Italians. At the age of 73, ʿUmar al-Mukhtar is therefore sentenced to death by hanging, and the sentence is carried out on September 15, 1931. The final scene, when ʿUmar al-Mukhtar's reading glasses drop from the gallows to the accompaniment of ululating howls of bereavement and fury on the part of all the Libyan prisoners of both sexes, is devastatingly done – whereas we are reminded that Graziani, to the contrary, was imprisoned for a short time in Italy after the death, also appropriately by hanging, of Mussolini in World War II, and was then himself released to die in 1955.

Although ʿUmar al-Mukhtar has long been regarded as a resistance hero by his own people, this film has, hopefully, converted him into a worldwide symbol of resistance to aggressive colonialist domination everywhere. Perhaps in one unexpected sense, however, it is just as well that Hollywood, by contrast, has produced so few good films about Muslim tribal resistance to colonialism: for it is thus a considerably less difficult task to separate known ethnographic or historical wheat from downright erroneous chaff (rather than perhaps the more ambitious headache of separating history from legend) than it is, for instance, in the enormous morass of bad films and dime novels about the once historical but now almost totally legendary sheriffs (as opposed to *sharif*-s) and bandits of the American West, such as the James and the Younger Brothers, Pat Garrett and Billy the Kid, Wild Bill Hickok, Doc Holliday and Wyatt Earp. In the light of this Qaddafi's deliberate suppression of the role of the Sanusiya order in the Libyan resistance to the Italians, once it is recognized, may not seem quite so bad. The fact remains, however, that as virtually the only one of the films here under review which is an unambiguously Hollywood production is 'The Wind and the Lion', containing, as it does, an unbelievable amount of factual error, the onetime cinematic and now television capital of Hollywood has, in our view, no reason whatsoever to congratulate itself. On the wider plane. the same is true of the whole Euro-American attitude toward Islam. Not only is this true of our persistent lack of cultural understanding of Islam, but of our downright hostility toward the faith of Islam and toward Muslims and Islamic civilization in general. As noted at the beginning of this study, Hollywood's treatment of Islam will win it no 'Oscars'; and despite the favorable commentary often echoed in this short study, I feel constrained to terminate my text on the same sombre and negative note on which it began. The literature may be somewhat better than the films, which are very bad indeed.

## Conclusion

The reader may well ask why I have chosen to spend so much time and effort on Middle Eastern and North African Muslim tribesmen in this study rather than on Middle Eastern and North African Muslims more generally, particularly when the former form such a small (and today, ever decreasing) percentage of the total population of the region. The answer is multiple: aside from the fact that I have a fuller personal knowledge of tribal areas and tribespeople, on the basis both of longer fieldworking time (in the Berber-speaking parts of Morocco and in the Pukhtun Tribal Agencies of the Pakistan North-West Frontier) and longer general exposure (to Bedouins both in Saudi Arabia and in the Western Sahara), than of urban ones, Middle Eastern tribesmen have always been far more important in the region at large than their mere numbers would suggest, in ways which either supported or ran counter to the aims of the central governments under whose tutelage they fell. Their freer, more colorful and more independent lifestyles, and their confidence in the stronger bonds of their own kinship and alliance systems, regardless of whether they are camel pastoralists or sedentary farmers, or whether they fall somewhere in between the two, for example, as sheep transhumants, have made them stand out more as societies (or, in terms of the nation-states to which they belong, part-societies) worthy of study in depth, both from a historical as well as an anthropological standpoint.

But the reactions that the various central governments concerned have had to these tribal societies vary as much, if not more, than do the societies themselves. The prevailing view is of course that tribalism and the tribal lifestyle and condition are retrogressive and that they must go. This is certainly the prevailing view in North Africa, particularly in Algeria albeit less stridently so in Morocco, and in much of the Middle East as well, although Saudi Arabia, Yemen, Afghanistan and the Pukhtun Tribal Agencies of Pakistan may be striking exceptions to this rule. Even so, the chances that Islamic Middle Eastern tribalism as it was once known in precolonial times will survive much longer, and even much past the twenty-first century, seem very remote indeed at the present time.

It goes without saying that of all factors most responsible for this state of affairs, Western colonialism must bear the heaviest brunt. The numerous examples both from the fiction of the colonizers themselves and, in particular, from that of native writers in the later post-colonial period – particularly those who have at last availed themselves of the chance to express themselves that they did not have beforehand, to say nothing of the films discussed subsequently – make this point abundantly clear. Indeed, in some cases colonial attitudes toward tribalism have merely been transferred to and readapted in only mildly different form by the governing elites of a good many postcolonial and independent states.

But (and a point which, as an American, I must stress) the cultural imperialism to which the USA in particular has fallen heir seems to die very hard, while the hidebound pre- and mis-conceptions of Hollywood in pandering to an audience which seems inevitably to prefer precooked and even predigested fare die hardest of all. But die they must, if our planet is ever truly to become 'One World'. One way to hasten that death is by trying to understand and to sympathize with the practitioners of other faiths, and with the cultures on which these faiths are embedded – in particular with Islam and with the beliefs and rituals of Muslims, who are nothing if not 'People of the Book', *ahl al-kitab* – rather than to sneer at them and to toss them aside merely because they are 'different' and 'not like us'. This is of course easier said than done; but as, at least in my own experience, the Muslim tribesman, in particular, tends to be a most likeable, engaging and genuine human being, with a strong sense of humor, an ingrained sense of hospitality and both a sense of forthrightness and a great fortitude in adversity, the effort seems to us to be well worth making, especially as his own normally rigid code of honor helps to ensure such behavior. I feel certain, furthermore, that he also wants to live at peace with the rest of the world, for *jihad*, much more than 'holy war', is essentially a question of self-improvement, and up to the present, at least, Islamism (or Islamic fundamentalism) has had little impact on tribesmen, who tend normally to be guided by pragmatism, more, perhaps, than by anything else.

# Bibliography

## *Works of Fiction Considered*

'Afghan' (Pseudonym)
   1922  *Exploits of Asaf Khan* (with foreword by Sir George Younghusband), London: Herbert Jenkins.
Aherdan, (Mahjoub)
   1991  *Un Poème pour Etendard*, Paris: Editions l'Harmattan.
Ali, Mohammad
   1966  *... And Then the Pathan Murders*, Peshawar: Khyber Bazaar.
Breem, Wallace
   1978  *The Leopard and the Cliff*, London: Methuen Magnum.
Cambra, de, Fernando P.
   1981  *Cuando Abd el-Krim Quiso Negociar con Franco*, Barcelona: Biblioteca Universal Caralt.
Chraibi, Driss
   1981  *Une Enquête au Pays*, Paris: Editions du Seuil.
   1982  *La Mère du Printemps (L'Oum er-Rbia)*, Paris: Editions du Seuil.
Coon, Carleton S.
   1932  *Flesh of the Wild Ox: A Riffian Chronicle of High Valleys and Long Rifles*, New York: William Morrow.
   1933  *The Riffian*, Boston: Little, Brown.
Euloge, René
   1951  *Silhouettes du Pays Chleuh*, Marrakech: Editions de la Tighermt.
   1952  *Les Derniers Fils de l'Ombre*, Marrakech: Editions de la Tighermt.
   1976  *Ceux des Hautes Vallées*, Marrakech: Editions de la Tighermt.
Feraoun, Mouloud
   1953  *La Terre et le Sang*, Paris: Editions du Seuil.
   1954  *Le Fils du Pauvre*, Paris; Editions du Seuil.
   1957  *Les Chemins qui montent*, Paris: Editions du Seuil.
   1962  *Journal, 1955-1962* (preface by Emmanuel Robles), Paris: Editions du Seuil.
   1969  *Lettres à ses Amis*, Paris: Editions du Seuil.
Hanley, Gerald
   1988  *The Consul at Sunset* (1951), London: André Deutsch.

Hirsh, M.E.
  1987  *Kabul*, London: Methuen.
Kemal, Yashar
  1981  *Memed My Hawk*, translated by Edmond Roditi (1961), London and New York: Writers and Readers.
Khair-Eddine, Mohammed
  1984  *Légende et Vie d'Agoun'chiche*, Paris: Editions du Seuil.
Khettouch, Moha ou Ali
  1991  *Azour Amokrane ne meurt jamais...*, Casablanca: Agence de Presse et d'Information.
Kipling, Rudyard
  1977  *Poems*, Harmondsworth, Middlesex: Penguin Poetry Library.
  1980  *Kim* (1901), London: Macmillan Pan.
  1987  *Selected Stories*, Harmondsworth, Middlesex: Penguin Books.
Layid, Moha
  1993  *Le Sacrifice des Vaches Noires*, Casablanca: Editions Eddif.
Le Glay, Maurice
  1930  *Les Sentiers de la Guerre et de l'Amour: Récit Marocain,* Paris: Berger-Levrault.
  1948  *Récits Marocains de la Plaine et des Monts* (1922), Paris: Berger-Levrault.
Mammeri, Mouloud
  1952  *La Colline Oubliée*, Paris: Librairie Plon.
  1955  *Le Sommeil du Juste*, Paris: Librairie Plon.
  1958  *The Sleep of the Just*, translated by Len Ortzen, Boston: Beacon Press.
  1965  *L'Opium et le Baton*, Paris: Presses Pocket/Librairie Plon.
Masters, John
  1956  *The Lotus and the Wind*, Harmondsworth, Middlesex: Penguin.
Michener, James
  1968  *Caravans*, New York: Random House, 1963, and Bantam.
Mirza, Youel B.
  1940  *Stripling*, New York: Wilfred Funk.
Mimouni, Rachid
  1989  *L'Honneur de la Tribu*, Paris: Robert Laffont.
Piersuis (Pseudonym)
  n.d.  *Bourrasque Bédouine*, Casablanca: Editions du Moghreb, n.d., but ca. 1935.
  1937  *Les Feux du Douar*, Casablanca: Editions du Moghreb.
  1947  *L'Oeil de Mahmoud*, Casablanca: Editions Antar.
Said, Kurban (Pseudonym)
  1971  *Ali and Nino*, translated by Jenia Graman, with introduction by John Wain, London: Arrow Books.
Shah, Idries
  1986  *KaraKush: The Gold of Ahmad Shah*, London: Collins.

## Other Sources Cited

Ahmed, Akbar S.
- 1977 *Social and Economic Change in the Tribal Areas, 1972-1976*, Karachi: Oxford University Press.
- 1991 *Resistance and Control in Pakistan*, (1983), with foreword by Francis Robinson, London and New York: Routledge.

Arnaud, Louis (MD)
- 1952 *Au Temps des Mehallas ou le Maroc de 1860 à 1912*, Institut des Hautes Etudes Marocaines, Notes et Documents, XII, Casablanca: Editions Atlantides.

Azoy, G. Whitney
- 1982 *Game and Power in Afghanistan*, Philadelphia: University of Pennsylvania Press.

Black-Michaud, Jacob
- 1986 *Sheep and Land: The Economics of Power in a Tribal Society*, Cambridge: Cambridge University Press, and Paris: Editions de la Maison des Sciences de l'Homme.

Burke, Edmund, III
- 1976 *Prelude to Protectorate in Morocco: Precolonial Protest and Resistance, 1860-1912*, Chicago and London: University of Chicago Press.

Coon, Carleton S.
- 1931 *Tribes of the Rif*, Harvard African Studies, IX, Cambridge, MA: Peabody Museum.
- 1962 *Caravan: The Story of the Middle East* (1951), 2nd Revised Ed., New York: Holt, Rinehart and Winston.
- 1981 *Adventures and Discoveries: The Autobiography of Carleton S. Coon*, Englewood Cliffs, NJ: Prentice-Hall.

Dugas, Guy
- 1985 'Politique Berbère et Littérature Berbériste du Maroc Colonial: Maurice Le Glay et Marie Barrère-Affre', *The Maghreb Review*, 10, 2-3, London 1985: 62-67.

Dunn, Ross E.
- 1977 *Resistance in the Desert: Moroccan Responses to French Imperialism, 1881-1912*, Madison: University of Wisconsin Press, and London: Croom Helm.

Dupree, Louis
- 1980 *Afghanistan*, (1973), 2nd Ed., Princeton, NJ: Princeton University Press.

Evans-Pritchard, E.E.
- 1971 *The Sanusi of Cyrenaica*, (1949), Oxford: Clarendon Press.

Forbes, Rosita
- 1924 *The Sultan of the Mountains: The Life Story of Raisuli*, New York: Henry Holt.

Gellner, Ernest
- 1969 *Saints of the Atlas*, London: Weidenfeld and Nicholson.
- 1984 'Doctor and Saint', in: Akbar S. Ahmed & David M. Hart (Eds.), *Islam in Tribal Societies: From the Atlas to the Indus*, London: Routledge and Kegan Paul: 21-38.

Hart, David M.
- 1976 *The Aith Waryaghar of the Moroccan Rif: An Ethnography and History*, Viking Fund Publications in Anthropology, No. 55, Tucson: University of Arizona Press.
- 1977 '"Assu u-Ba Slam (1890-1960): De la Résistance à la "Pacification" au Maroc (essai d'Anthropologie Sociale)', in: Charles-André Julien, Magali Morsy, Catherine Cocquery-Vidrovitch & Yves Person (Eds.), *Les Africains*, Paris: Editions Jeune Afrique, vol. 5, pp. 75-105.
- 1981 *Dadda ʿAtta and his Forty Grandsons: The Socio-Political Organisation of the Ait ʿAtta of Southern Morocco*, Wisbech, Cambridgeshire: Menas Press.
- 1984 *The Ait ʿAtta of Southern Morocco: Daily Life and Recent History*, Wisbech, Cambridgeshire: Menas Press.
- 1985 *Guardians of the Khaibar Pass: The Social Organization and History of the Afridi of Pakistan*, with foreword by Akbar S. Ahmed, Lahore: Vanguard Books.
- 1987 *Banditry in Islam: Case Studies from Morocco, Algeria and the Pakistan North-West Frontier*, Menas Studies in Continuity and Change, Wisbech, Cambridgeshire: Menas Press.
- 1990 'The Afridi of the Khaibar Tribal Agency and the Kohat Frontier Region', in: Ahmed, Akbar S. (Ed.), *Pakistan: The Social Sciences' Perspective*, Karachi: Oxford University Press, pp. 1-27.
- 1994 'Conflits Extérieurs et Vendettas dans le Djurdjura Algérien et le Rif Marocain', *Awal: Cahiers d'Etudes Berbères* 11: 95-122.
- 1997a *Estructuras Tribales Precoloniales en Marruecos Bereber, 1860-1933: Una Reconstruccion Etnografica en Perspectiva Historica*, Granada: Universidad de Granada/Diputacion Provincial de Granada.
- 1997B 'The Berber Dahir of 1930 in Colonial Morocco: Then and Now (1930-1996)', *Journal of North African Studies* 2(2): 11-33.

Hobsbawm, E. J.
- 1972 *Bandits*, (1969), 2nd Ed., Harmondsworth, Middlesex: Penguin.

Khatibi, Abdelkabir
- 1968 *Le Roman Maghrébin*, Paris: François Maspéro.

Kilborne, Benjamin
- 1978 *Interprétations du Rêve au Maroc*, in series ed. by Georges Devereux, Bibliothèque d'Ethnopsychiatrie, Paris: La Pensée Sauvage.

Lahjomri, Abdeljlil
- 1973 *L'Image du Maroc dans la Littérature Française (de Loti à Montherlant)*, Etudes et Documents, Algiers: Société Nationale d'Edition et de Diffusion (SNED).

Marcy, Georges
  1936 'L'Alliance par Co-lactation (*tad'a*) chez les Berbères du Maroc Central', in: *Deuxième Congres de la Fédération des Sociétés Savantes de l'Afrique du Nord*, Algiers 1936, II, 2: 957-973.
Pennell, C.R.
  1986 *A Country with a Government and a Flag: the Rif War in Morocco, 1921-1926*, Wisbech, Cambridgeshire: Menas Press.
Prochaska, David
  1986 'Fire on the Mountain: Resisting Colonialism in Algeria', in: Donald Crummey (Ed.), *Banditry, Rebellion and Social Protest in Africa*, London: James Currey, and Portsmouth, NH: Heinemann, pp. 229-252.
Rodinson, Maxime
  1976 *Mohammed*, translated by Anne Carter, Harmondsworth, Middlesex: Pelican Books.
Trench, Charles Chevenix
  1986 *The Frontier Scouts*, London: Jonathan Cape.
Tuchman, Barbara W.
  1984 'Perdicaris Alive or Raisuli Dead', in idem, *Practising History*, London: Macmillan, pp. 104-117.
Watt, W. Montgomery
  1961 *Muhammad: Prophet and Statesman*, Oxford: Oxford University Press.